PIANO • VOCAL • GUITAR

# RED HOT CHILI PEPPERS
## I'M WITH YOU

ISBN 978-1-4584-1878-4

HAL•LEONARD®
CORPORATION
7777 W. BLUEMOUND RD. P.O. BOX 13819 MILWAUKEE, WI 53213

In Australia Contact:
Hal Leonard Australia Pty. Ltd.
4 Lentara Court
Cheltenham, Victoria, 3192 Australia
Email: ausadmin@halleonard.com.au

Visit Hal Leonard Online at
**www.halleonard.com**

# MONARCHY OF ROSES

Words and Music by ANTHONY KIEDIS,
FLEA, CHAD SMITH
and JOSH KLINGHOFFER

Do you like ___ it rough, ___ I ___ ask, ___ and
cross be - tween ___ my for - mer ___ queen, ___ her

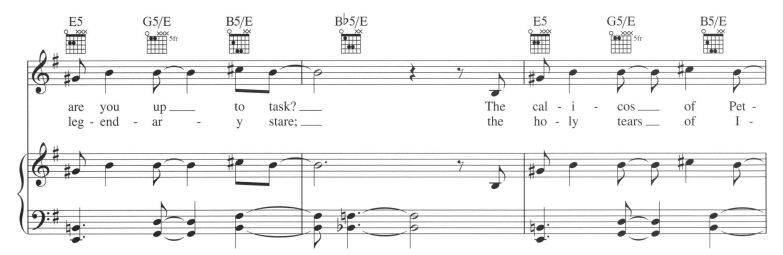

are you up ___ to task? ___ The cal - i - cos ___ of Pet -
leg - end - ar - y stare; ___ the ho - ly tears ___ of I -

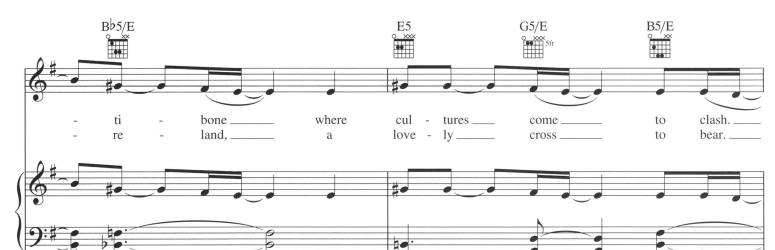

- ti - bone _____ where cul - tures ___ come _____ to clash. ___
- re - land, _____ a love - ly ___ cross _____ to bear. ___

(1., D.S.) Sev -'ral of ___ my best ___ friends wear ___ the
(2.) Sev -'ral of ___ my best ___ friends know ___ the

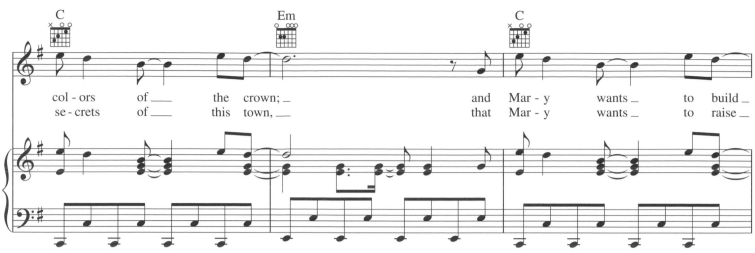

col - ors of \_\_\_ the crown; \_\_\_ and Mar - y wants \_\_ to build \_\_
se - crets of \_\_\_ this town, \_\_\_ that Mar - y wants \_\_ to raise \_\_

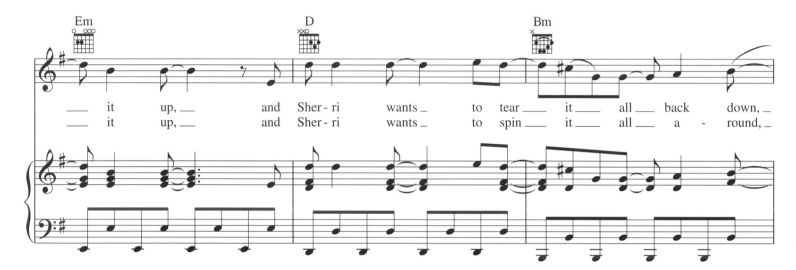

\_\_ it up, \_\_ and Sher - ri wants \_\_ to tear \_\_ it \_\_ all \_\_ back down, \_\_
\_\_ it up, \_\_ and Sher - ri wants \_\_ to spin \_\_ it \_\_ all \_\_ a - round, \_\_

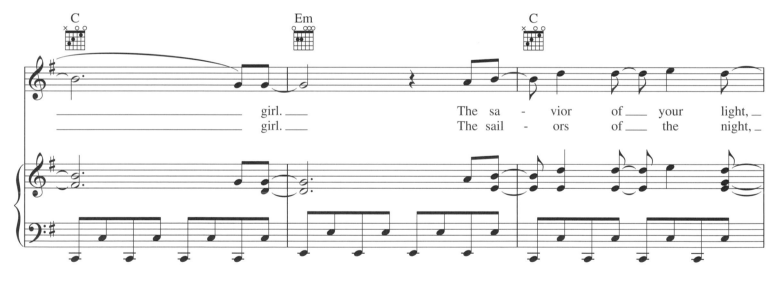

_____ girl. \_\_ The sa - vior of \_\_ your light, \_\_
_____ girl. \_\_ The sail - ors of \_\_ the night, \_\_

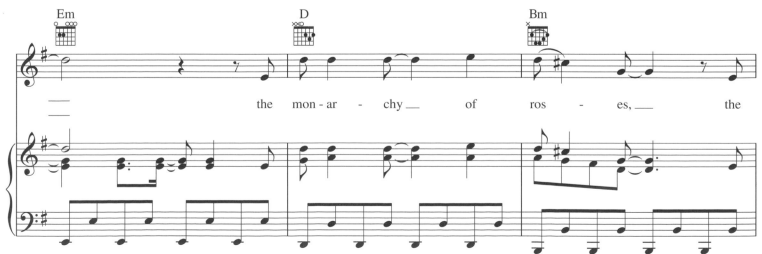

\_\_ the mon - ar - chy \_\_ of ros - es, \_\_ the

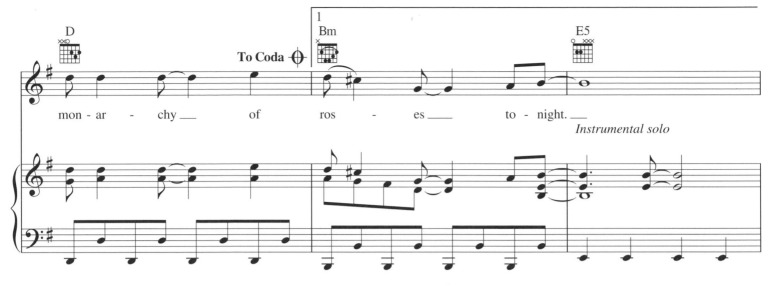

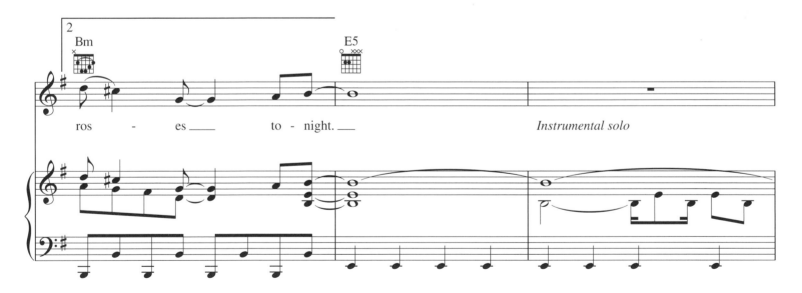

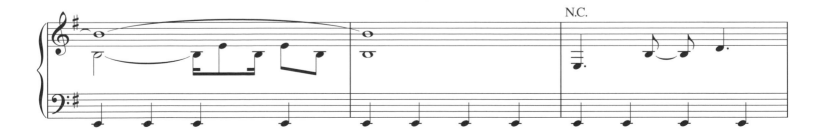

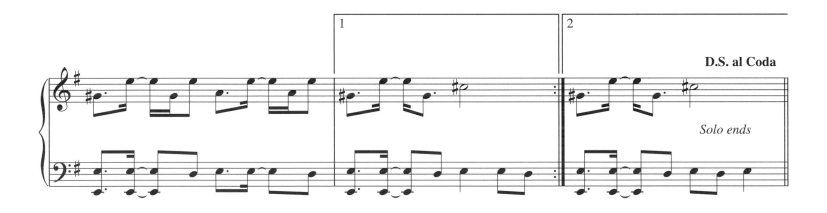

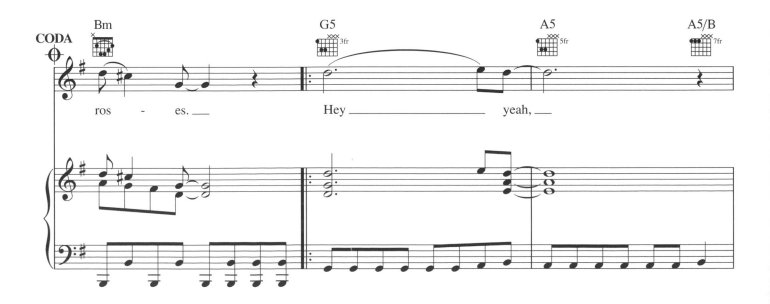

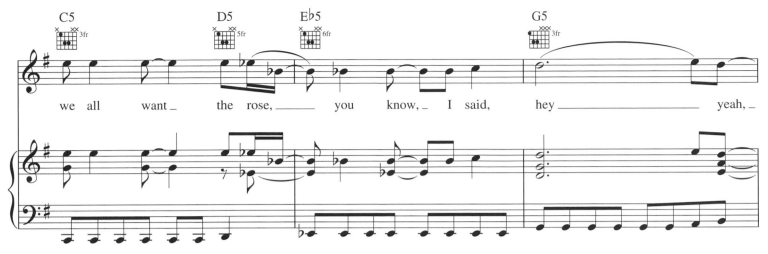

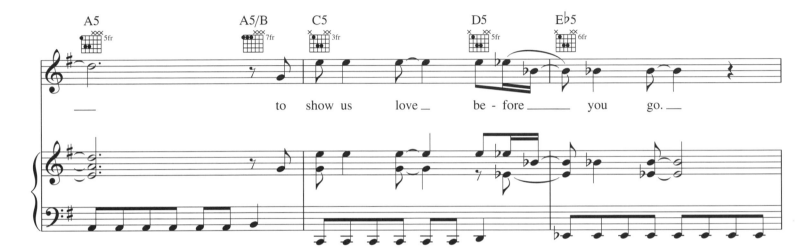

# FACTORY OF FAITH

Words and Music by ANTHONY KIEDIS,
FLEA, CHAD SMITH
and JOSH KLINGHOFFER

**Moderately fast Rock**

All my life, I was swing-ing for the fence; I was look-ing for the trip-le, nev-er

play-ing good de-fense. Gun-nin' for the glit-ter, ev-'ry hot and heav-y hit-ter. She was

nev - er real - ly there, so I could - n't real - ly get her. Said, Fac - tu - al - ly, I,

I'm just a piece of it. Fac - tu - al - ly, I, the ver - y least of it.

Piece of work; I was real - ly quite a jerk. Keep-ing score is such a bore, a bus - y
Crack your whip, she's con - fess-ing from the hip. She was good at get-ting there, but not as

mind could go be - serk, oh. Feast on this: I was fish - ing for a hook, so I
much for round - trip, oh. All this time, I was search-ing for a dream. I was

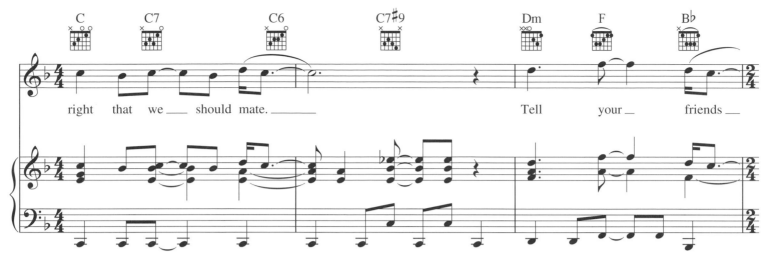

right that we ____ should mate. _____ Tell your __ friends __

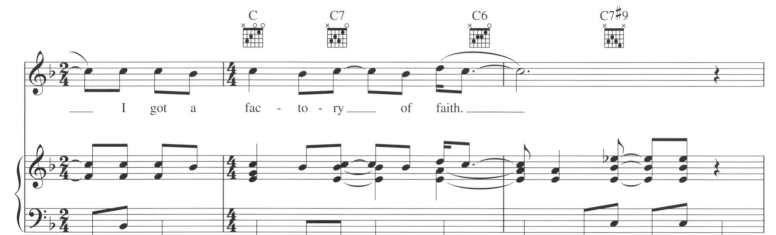

__ I got a fac - to - ry ____ of faith. _____

Late last ____ night, _____ I had a dream that it ____ was great. ____

**To Coda** ⊕

____ Tell your __ friends _____ I've got a fac - to - ry ____ of faith,

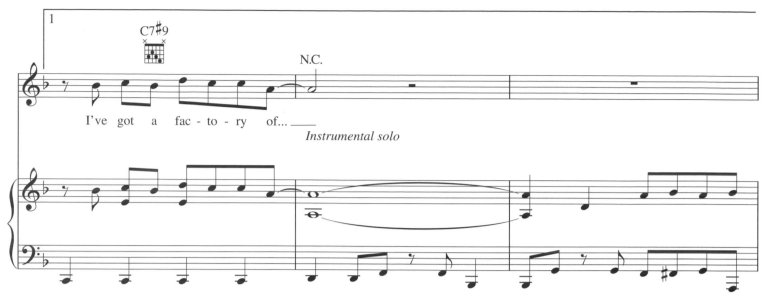

I've got a fac-to-ry of... _____

*Instrumental solo*

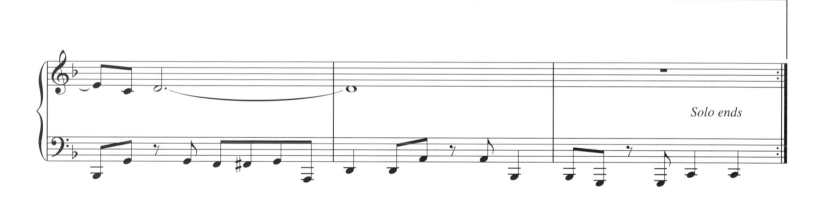

*Solo ends*

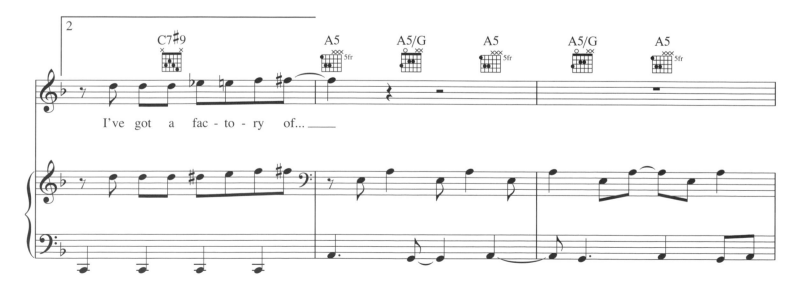

I've got a fac-to-ry of... _____

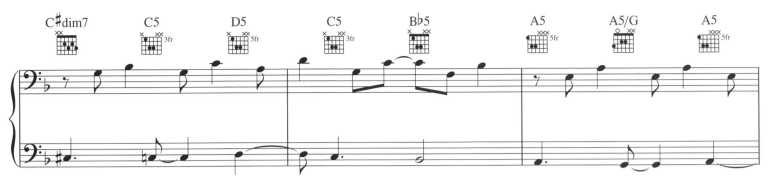

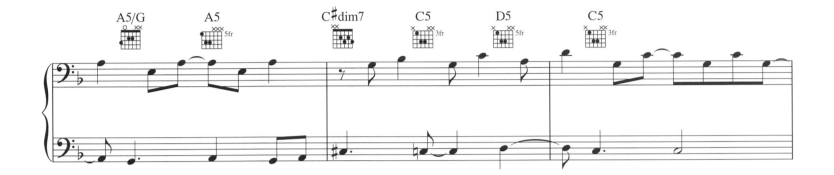

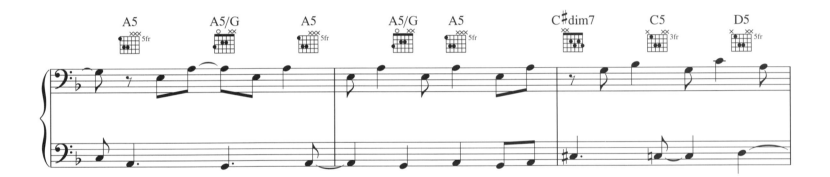

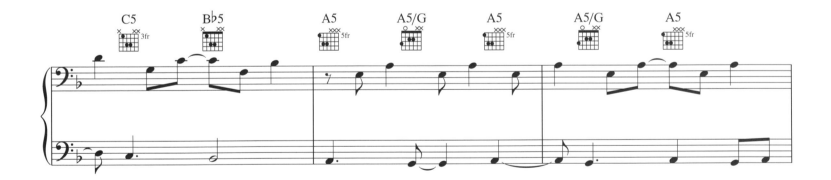

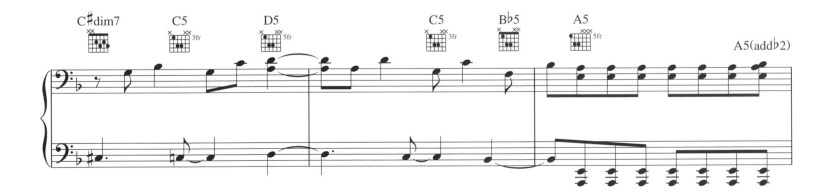

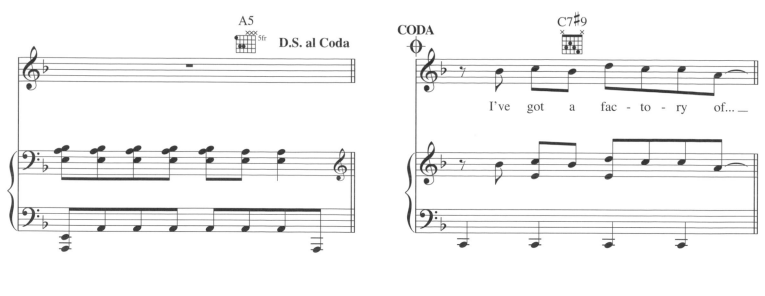

D.S. al Coda

CODA

I've got a fac - to - ry of... __

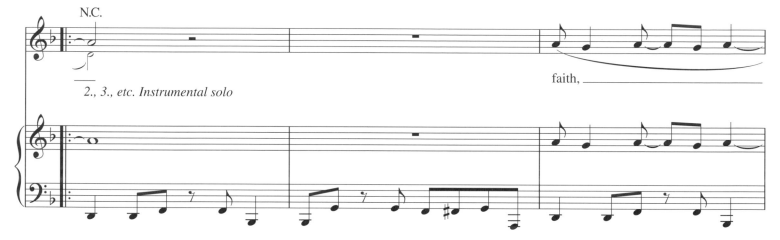

2., 3., etc. Instrumental solo

faith, _____

and love, _____ and

**Repeat ad lib.**    **Final Ending**

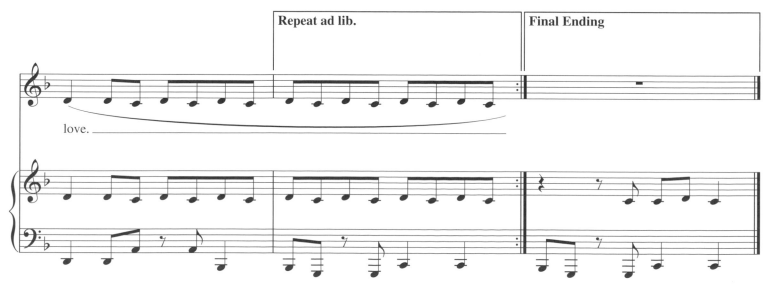

love. _____

# BRENDAN'S DEATH SONG

Words and Music by ANTHONY KIEDIS,
FLEA, CHAD SMITH
and JOSH KLINGHOFFER

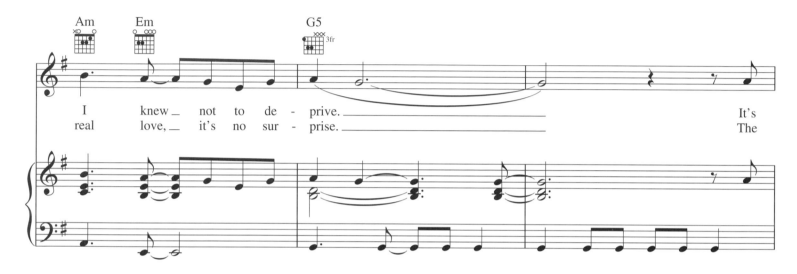

love su - preme,_ you are the rise._____ And when you
be a - gain;_ it was a time._____ It's gon - na

hear this,____ you know it's your jam,____ it's your good -
catch you;___ so glad I met you____ to walk the

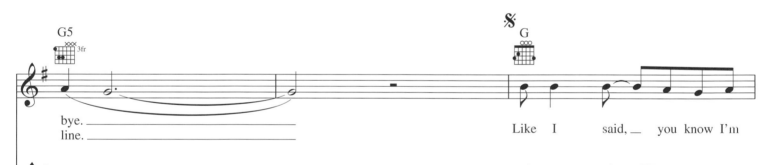

bye.____ Like I said,_ you know I'm
line.____

al - most dead,_ you know I'm al - most gone;_____ and when the

drum - mer drums, _ he's going to play my song _ to car - ry

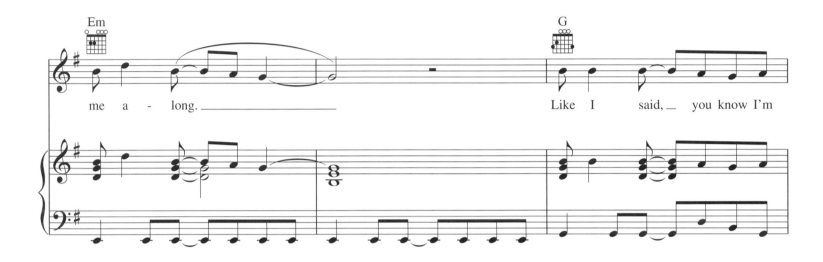

me a - long. _____ Like I said, _ you know I'm

al - most dead, _ you know I'm al - most gone; _____ and when the

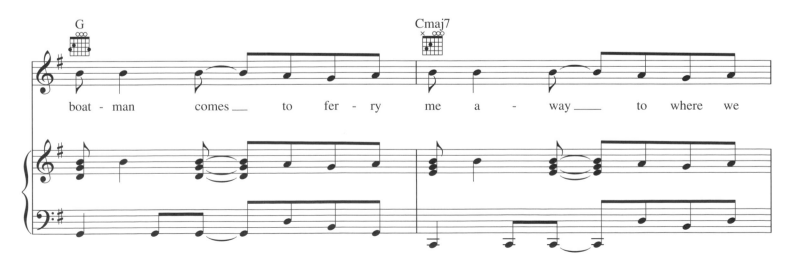

boat - man comes _ to fer - ry me a - way _ to where we

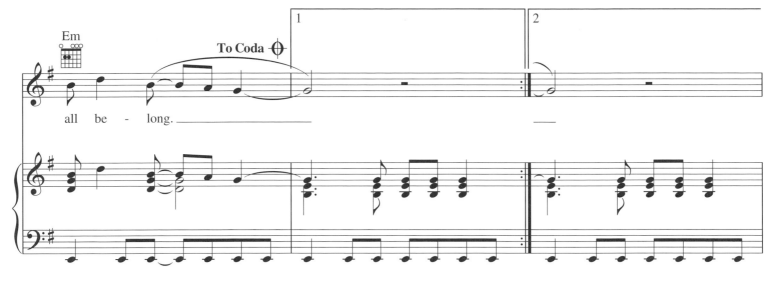

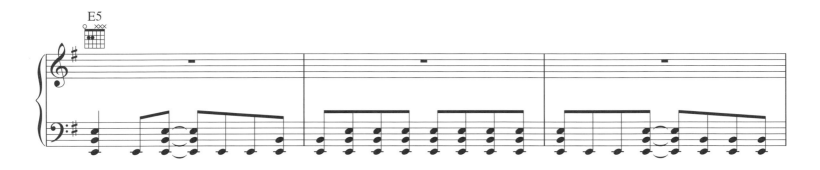

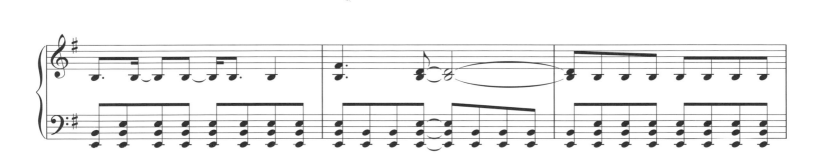

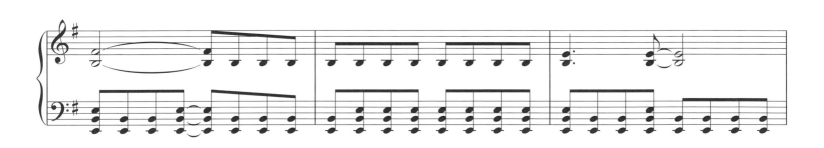

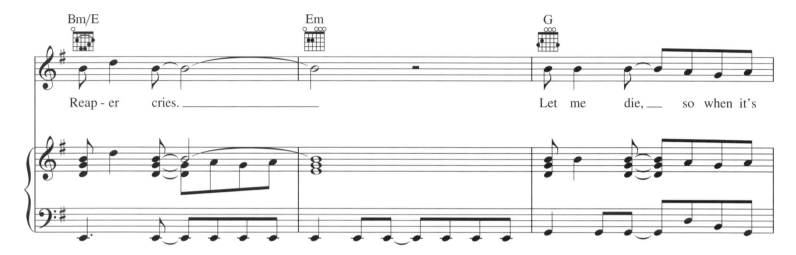

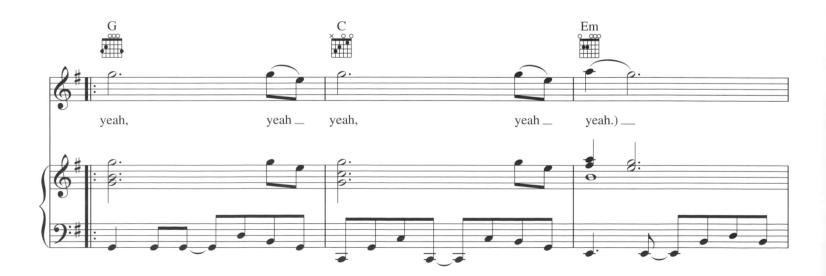

# ETHIOPIA

Words and Music by ANTHONY KIEDIS,
FLEA, CHAD SMITH
and JOSH KLINGHOFFER

E I O I E I A, ___ when you give your love ___ a - way, you get a ___

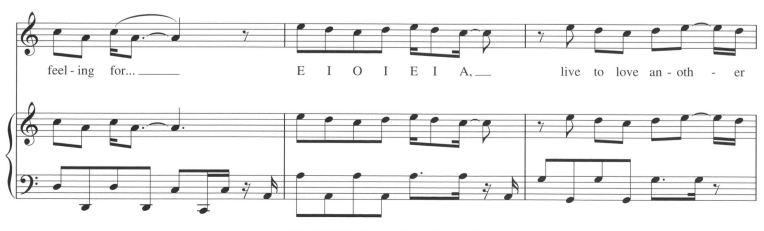

feel-ing for... ___ E I O I E I A, ___ live to love an - oth - er

day, e - ven when you feel un - sure._____ More_ and

more I wan - na raise,_____ raise_ my bar and raise____ your stakes._

E I O I E I A,____ when I lie there wide_____ a-

wake, for my_____ son I'll make._ Tell_

Am

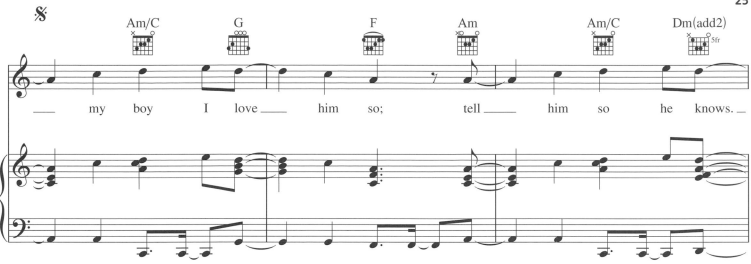

my boy I love ___ him so; tell ___ him so he knows. ___

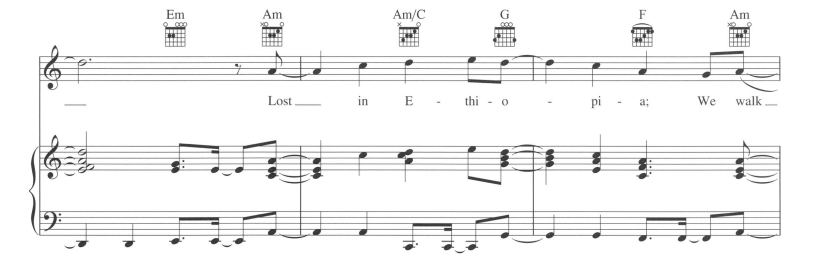

___ Lost ___ in E - thi - o - pi - a; We walk ___

**To Coda** ⊕

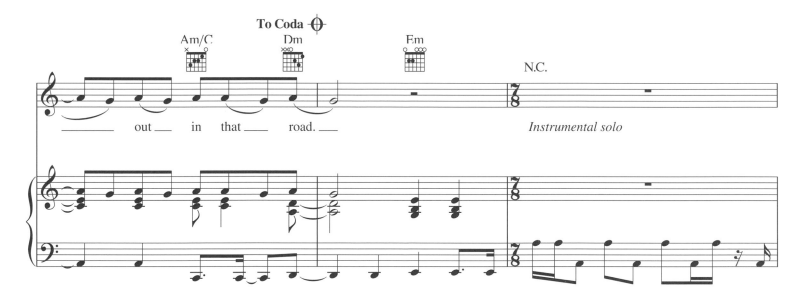

___ out ___ in that ___ road. ___ N.C.

*Instrumental solo*

*Solo ends*

26

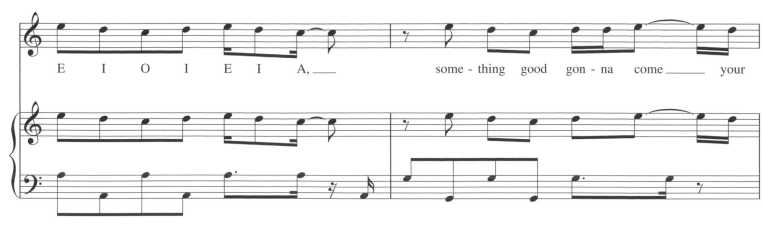

E I O I E I A, \_\_\_\_ some-thing good gon-na come \_\_\_\_\_ your

way; just \_\_\_\_ look out your door. \_\_\_\_\_

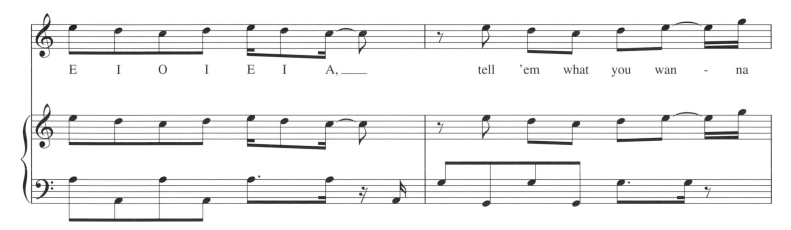

E I O I E I A, \_\_\_\_ tell 'em what you wan-na

**D.S. al Coda**

Am

say, no mat-ter \_\_\_\_ what you might in-cur. \_\_\_\_ Tell \_\_\_

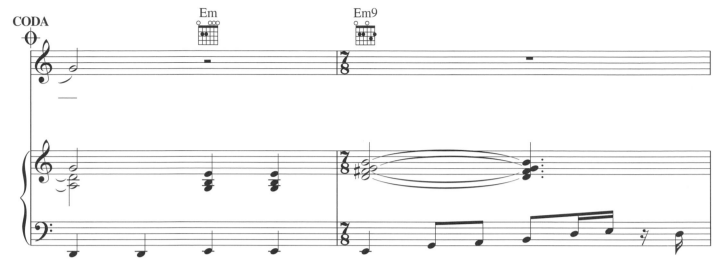

28

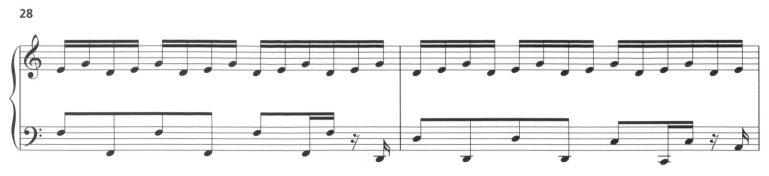

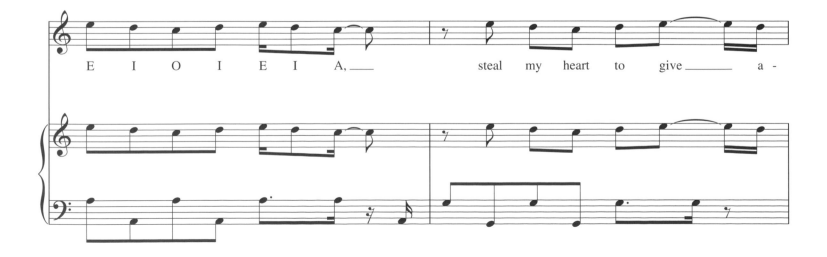

E    I    O    I    E    I    A, _____          steal  my  heart  to  give _____  a -

way, make me _ want to say,                     E  I  O  I  E  I  A, _

you and I are sewn    the    same, _____

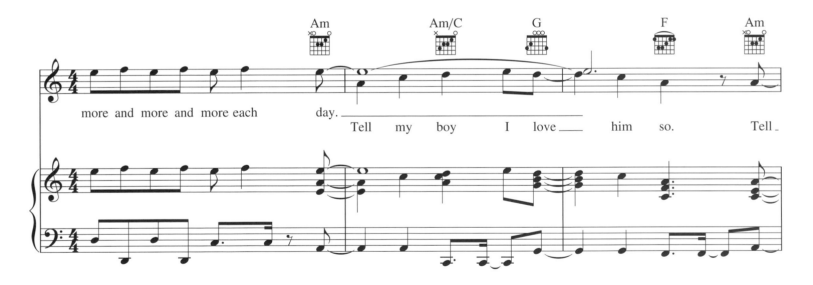

more and more and more each    day. _____    Tell my boy I love ___ him so.        Tell _

_ him so he knows. ___                         Lost ___ in E - thi - o -

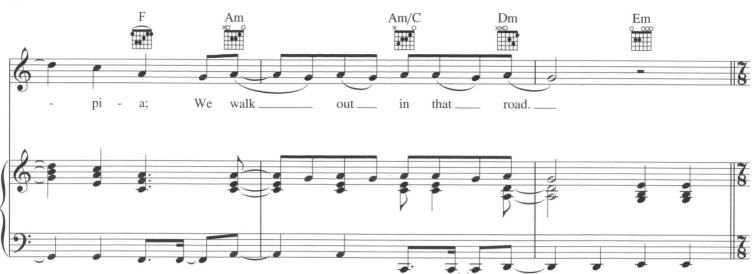

# ANNIE WANTS A BABY

Words and Music by ANTHONY KIEDIS,
FLEA, CHAD SMITH
and JOSH KLINGHOFFER

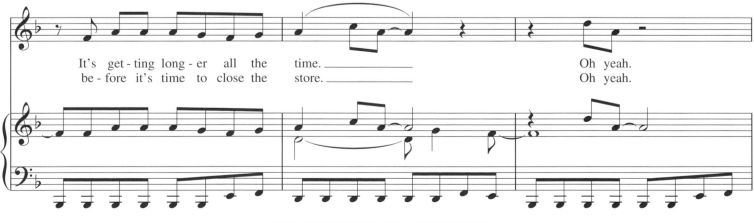

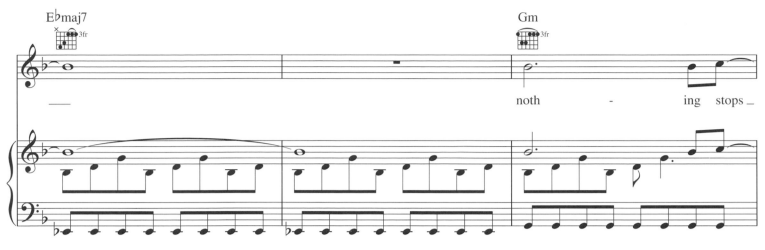

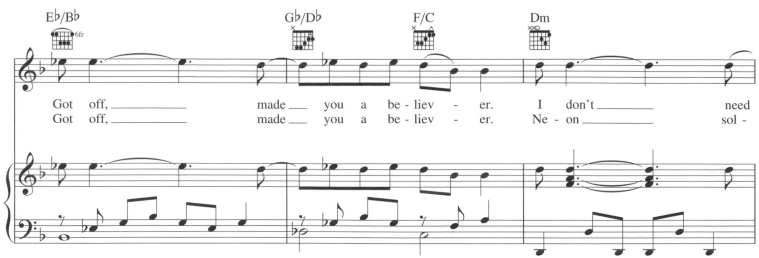

Got off, _____ made __ you a be - liev - er. I don't _____ need
Got off, _____ made __ you a be - liev - er. Ne - on _____ sol -

___ to _____ ten - der, _____ why __ do I be - lieve _ you?
- dier _____ left her, _____ now __ you've got - ten old - er.

An - nie wants a ba - by now. ___ An - nie wants a ba - by

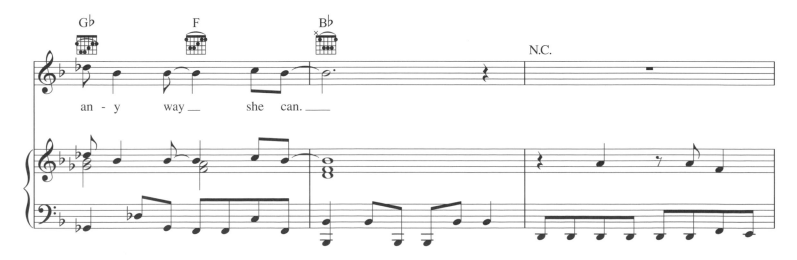

an - y way __ she can. ___

It's get-ting long-er all the time._____

It's time to re - de - sign the sign._____ Oh yeah.

Gm          F(add2)          E♭maj7

Sings          a - long ____          the way... _____

# LOOK AROUND

Words and Music by ANTHONY KIEDIS,
FLEA, CHAD SMITH
and JOSH KLINGHOFFER

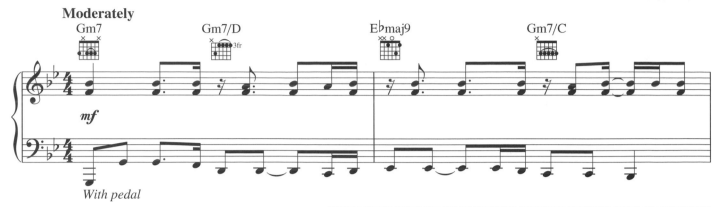

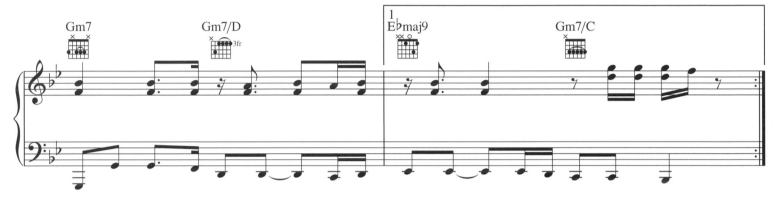

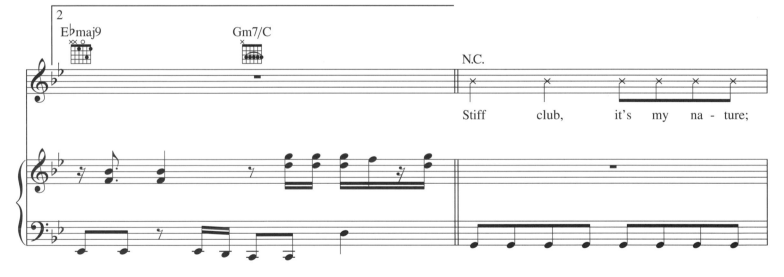

Stiff club, it's my na-ture; cus-tom love is the no-men-cla-ture. Turn down mass con-fu-sion.

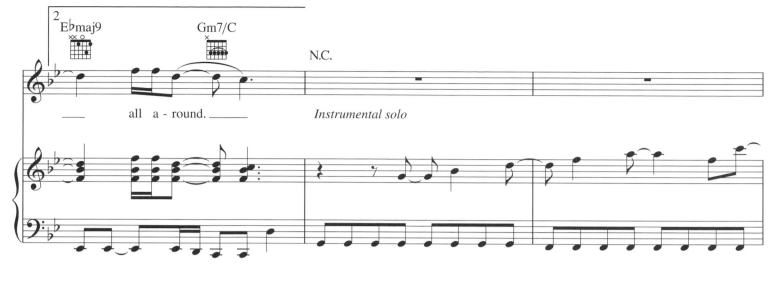

all a - round. *Instrumental solo*

*Solo ends* It's e - mo - tion - al,

and I told __ you so, but you had __ to know, so I told __ you.

Please don't look right through me; hurts my heart when you do that to me.

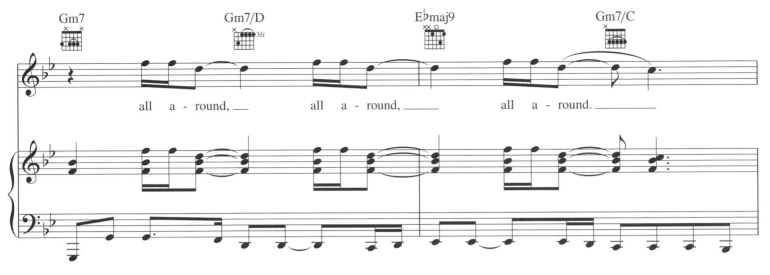

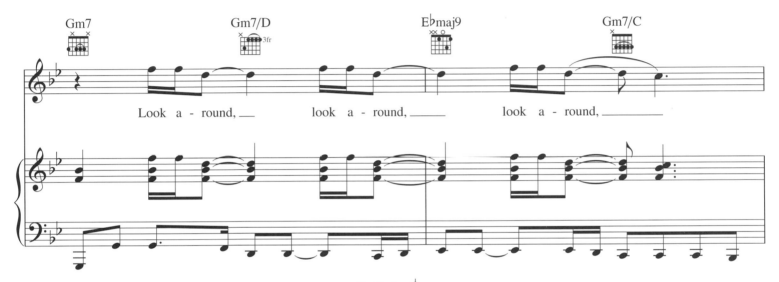

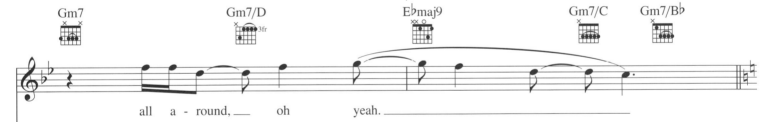

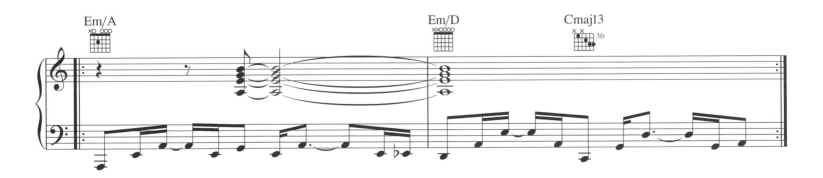

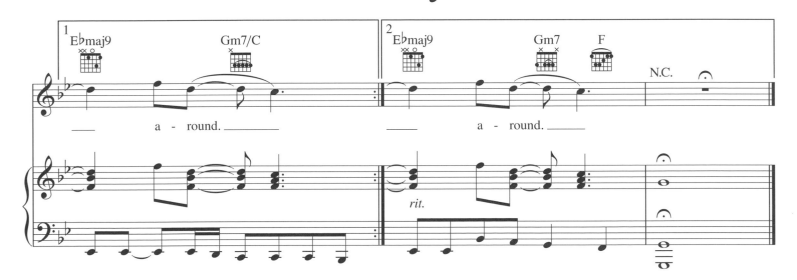

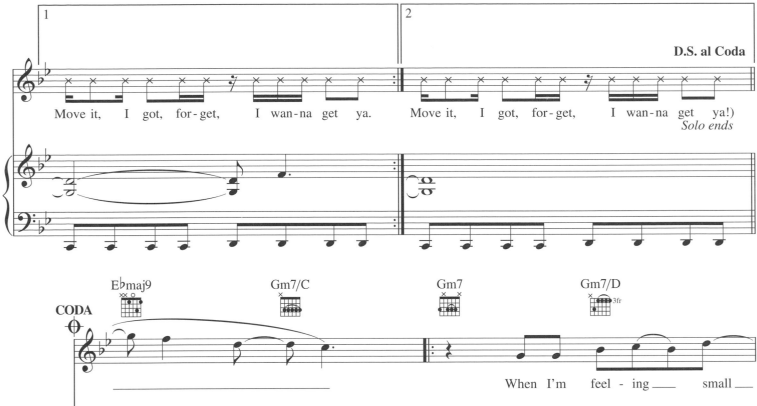

# THE ADVENTURES OF RAIN DANCE MAGGIE

Words and Music by ANTHONY KIEDIS,
FLEA, CHAD SMITH
and JOSH KLINGHOFFER

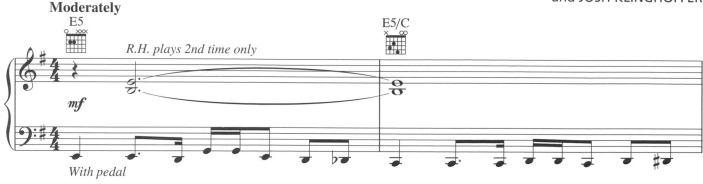

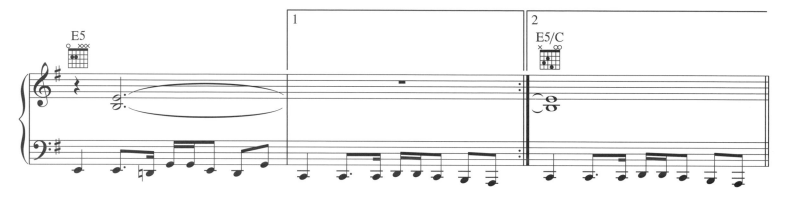

Lip-stick junk-ie, de-bunk___ the all in one, she came back wear-ing a smile.___

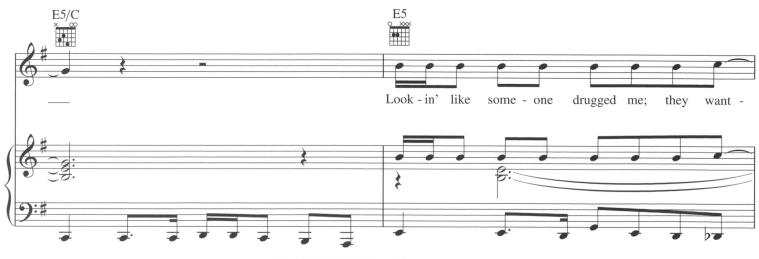

___ Look-in' like some-one drugged me; they want-

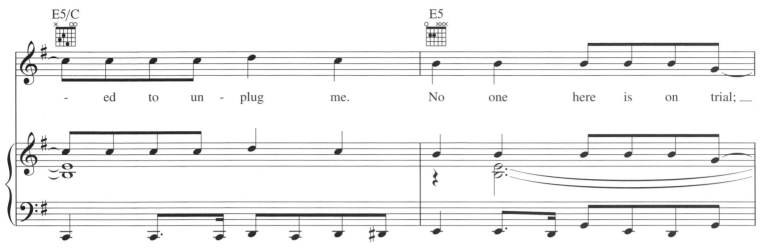

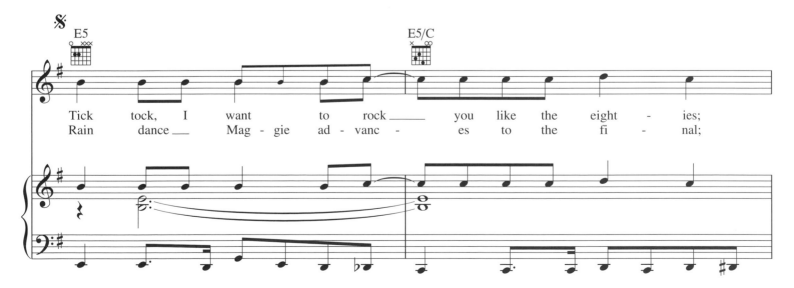

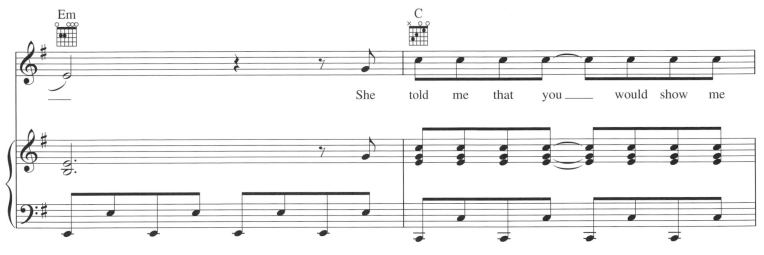

She told me that you ___ would show me

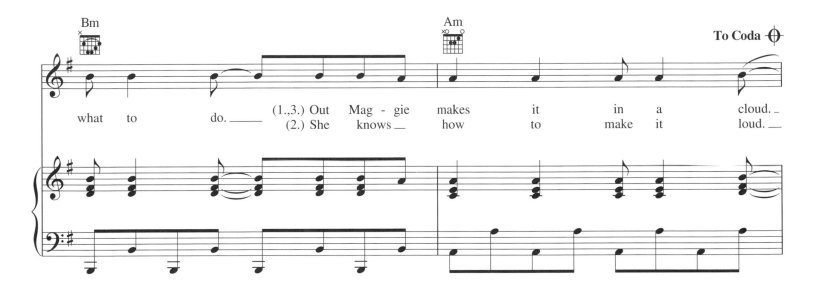

To Coda ⊕

what to do. ___ (1.,3.) Out Mag - gie makes it in a cloud. ___
(2.) She knows ___ how to make it loud. ___

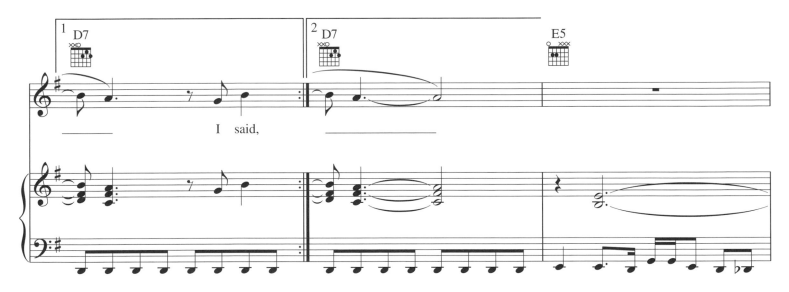

I said,

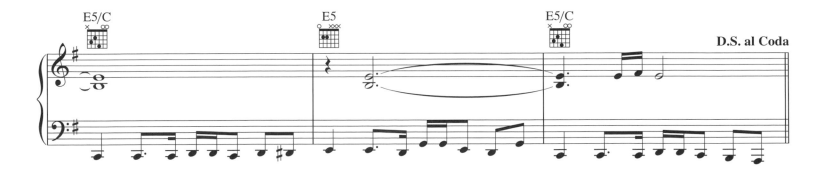

D.S. al Coda

48

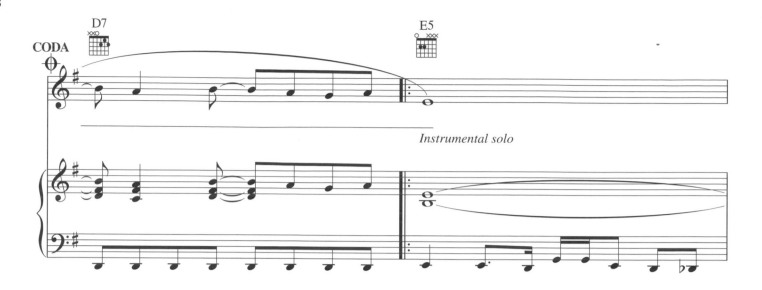

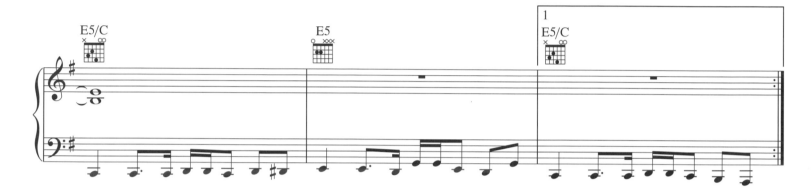

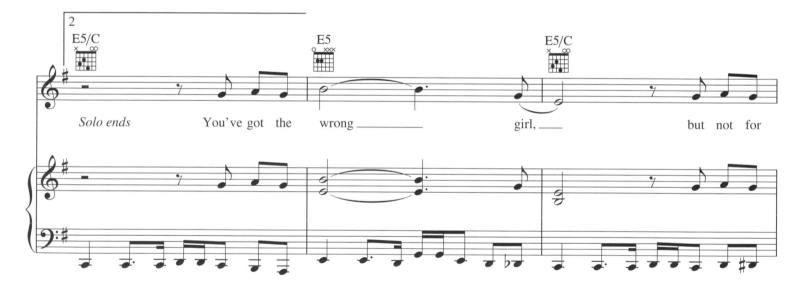

Solo ends    You've got the wrong _____ girl, _____ but not for

long, _____ girl. _____ It's in the song, _____ girl, _

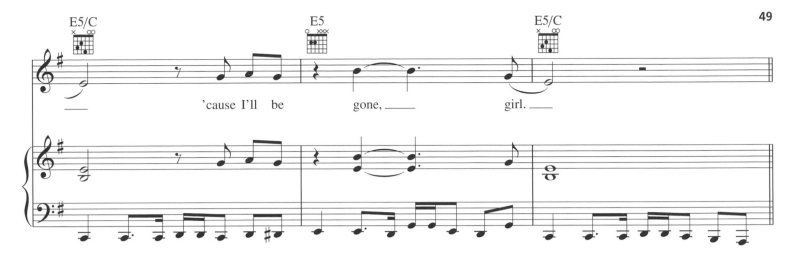

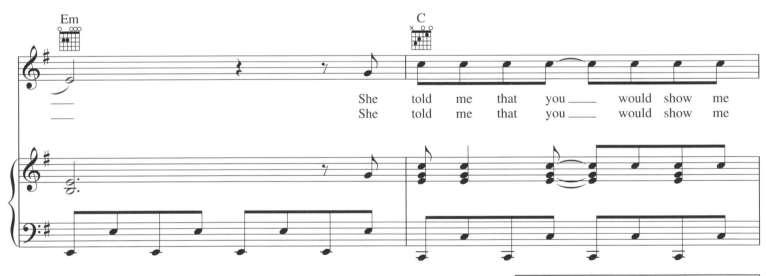

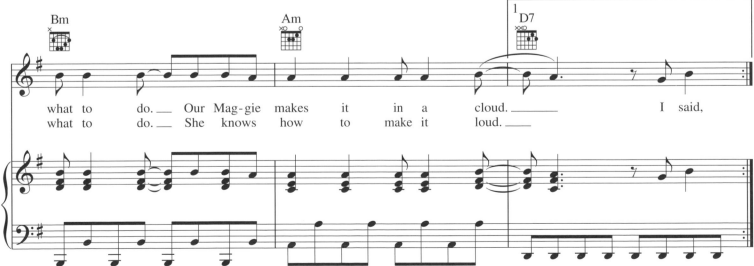

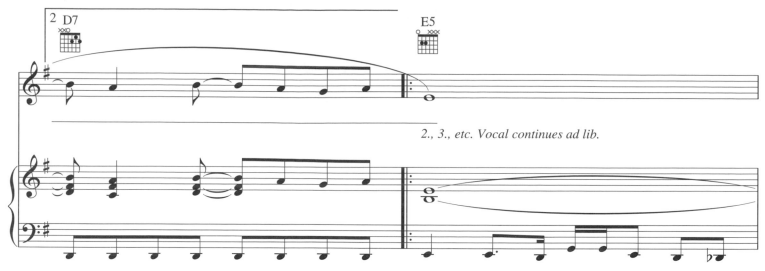

*2., 3., etc. Vocal continues ad lib.*

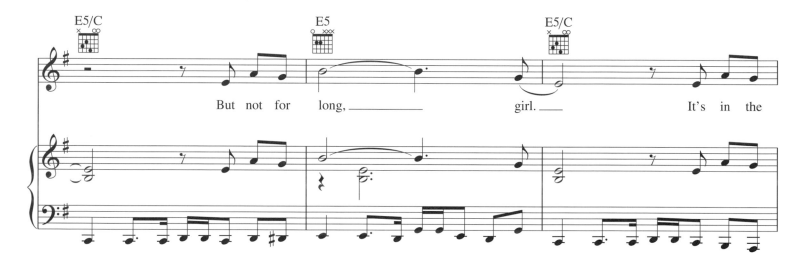

But not for long, _____ girl. ___ It's in the

song, _____ girl, ___ 'cause I'll be gone, bye bye bye, __ yeah. __

**Repeat ad lib.**          **Final Ending**

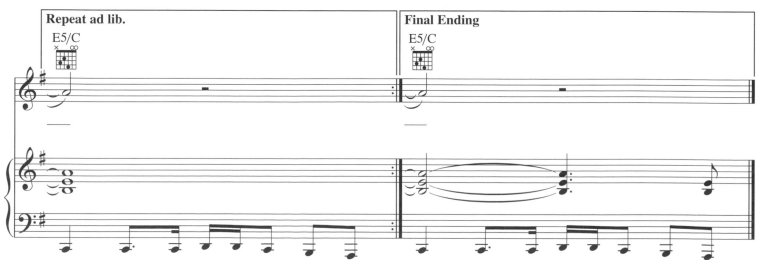

# DID I LET YOU KNOW

Words and Music by ANTHONY KIEDIS,
FLEA, CHAD SMITH
and JOSH KLINGHOFFER

**Moderate Rock, with a groove**

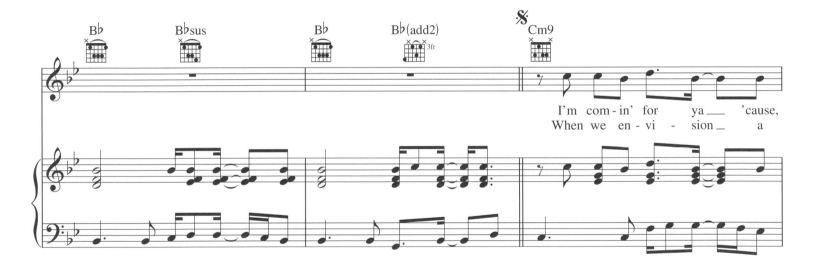

I'm com-in' for ya ___ 'cause,
When we en - vi - sion ___ a

'cause I a - dore ya ___ and I'd like to get in - side your mass pro - duc - tion.
lack of di - vi - sion ___ and the plan - et does an - oth - er re - vo - lu - tion.

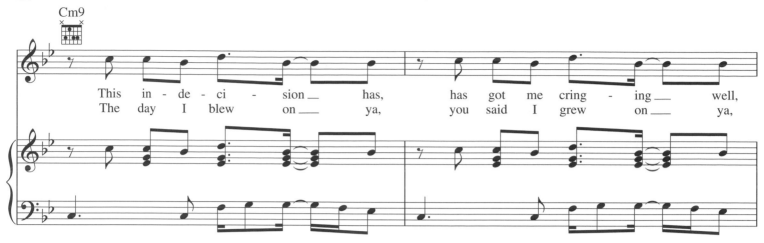

Did I let __ you know?    Would you like __ to go?

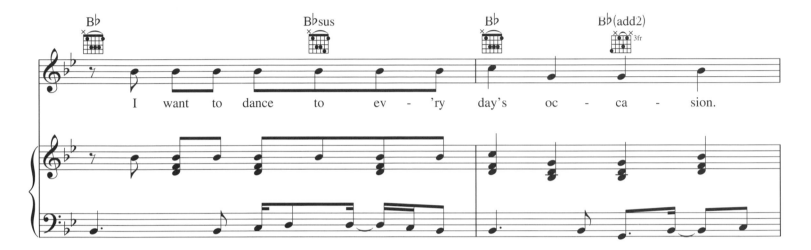

I want to dance to ev - 'ry day's oc - ca - sion.

This I __ know, yeah, this I __ know. _____ Take me __ home, __ well, __

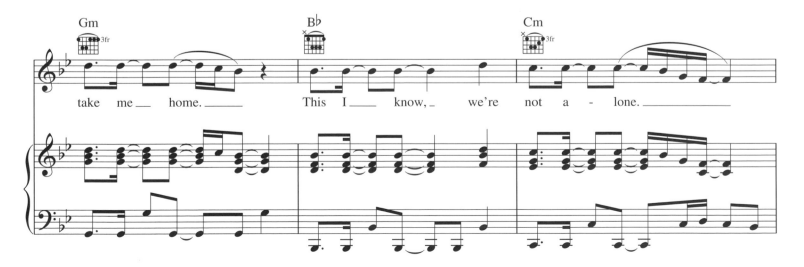

take me __ home. _____ This I __ know, __ we're not a - lone. _____

54

Take me ___ home, ___ take me ___ home. ___

D.S. al Coda

one so - lu - tion. Go!

*trumpet solo*

I'm com-ing at you __ well, year of the cat too __ and

I like the sound of your ar-ti-cu-la-tions.

Want to a-rouse her, __ and may-be es-pouse her, __ well,

she showed me love with-out the stip-u-la-tions.

56

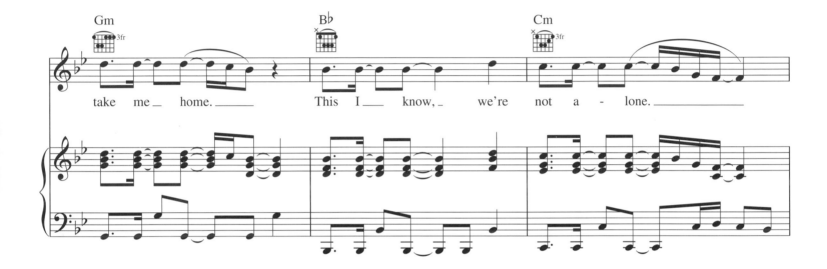

guitar solo

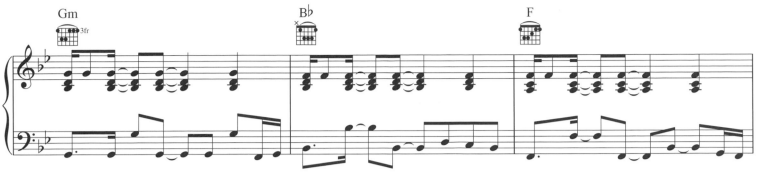

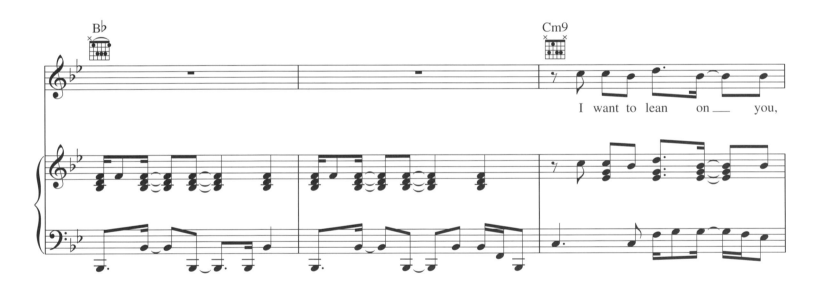

I want to lean on ___ you,

get Jan and Dean on ___ you. It's time to sway a lit - tle

not a - lone._____ Take me __ home, __ take me __ home. _

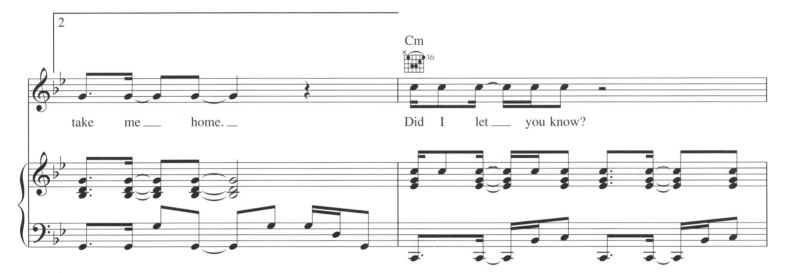

take me ___ home. __ Did I let ___ you know?

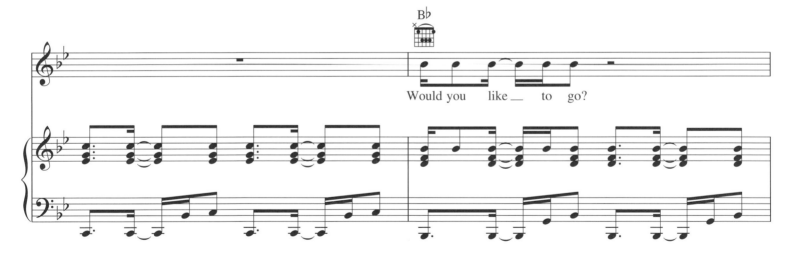

Would you like __ to go?

Did I let ___ you know? _____

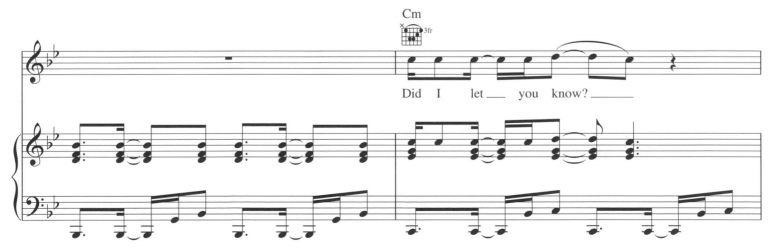

And would you like __ to go. _____

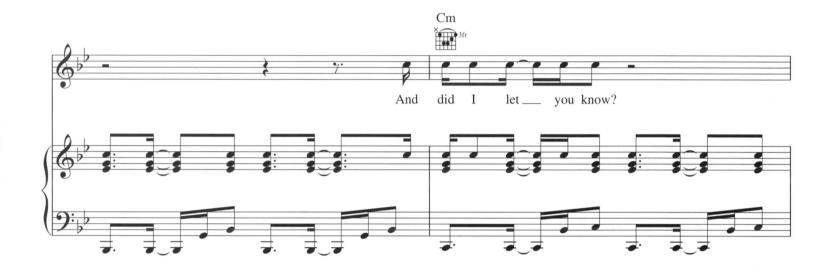

And did I let __ you know?

And would you like __ to go? _____

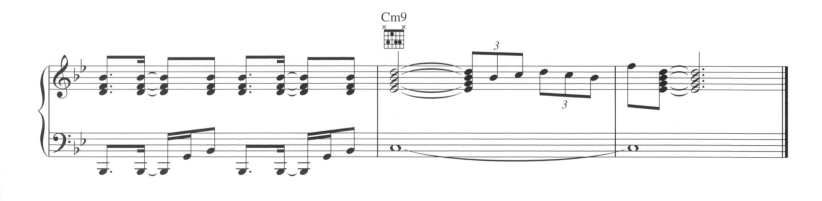

# GOODBYE HOORAY

Words and Music by ANTHONY KIEDIS,
FLEA, CHAD SMITH
and JOSH KLINGHOFFER

**Driving Rock**

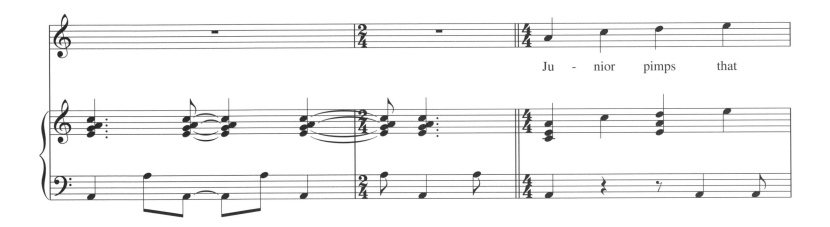

Ju - nior pimps that old ca - fe, ___ got to change those girls a - round. ___

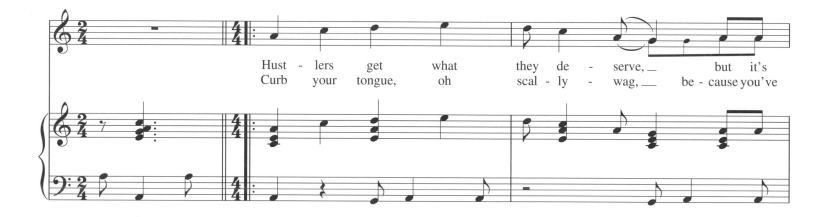

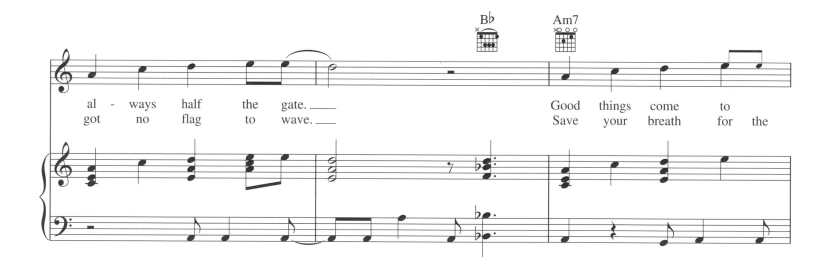

See you a - round, I'll see you a - round, I'll play all night, can't

get up - tight. I will lead all your mind games a -

stray. Well, I'll see you a - round, I'll

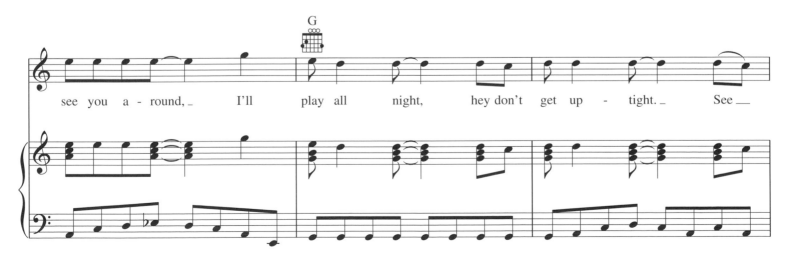

see you a - round, I'll play all night, hey don't get up - tight. See

you, so \_\_\_ long, \_ good - bye, \_ hoo - ray. _____

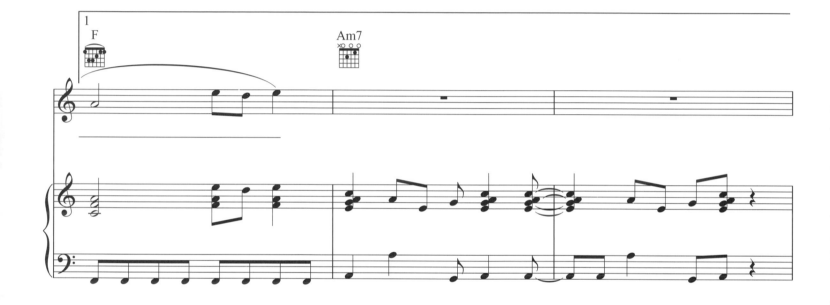

Well, I'll see you a - round, I'll see you a - round. ____

*vocal tacet on repeat*

*bass solo*

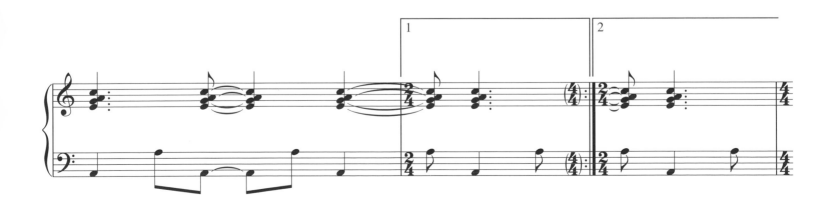

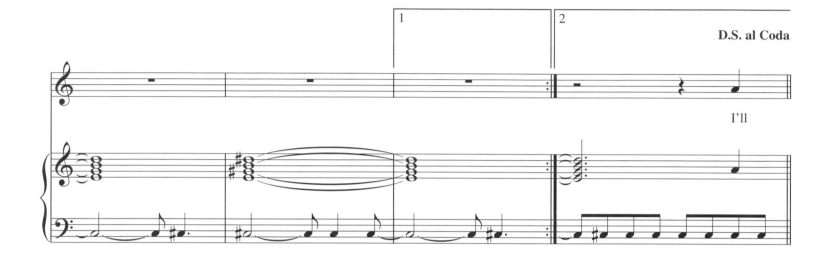

D.S. al Coda

I'll

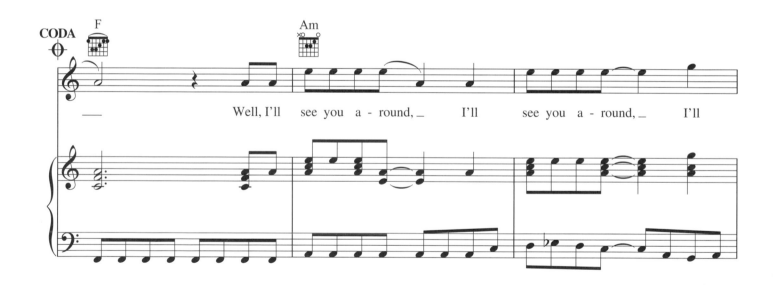

CODA

Well, I'll see you a - round, __ I'll see you a - round, __ I'll

see you a - round, __ I'll see you a - round. __ I'll see you a - round, __ good -

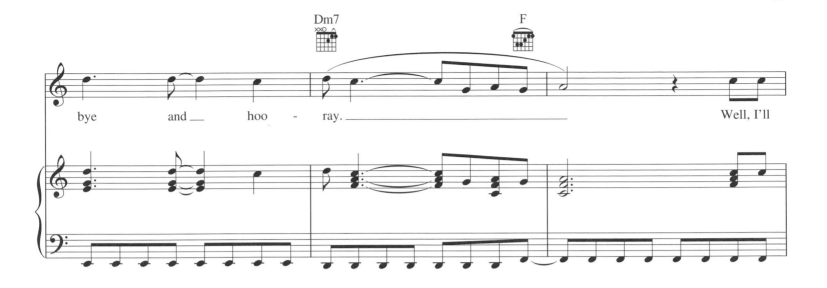

bye and ___ hoo - ray. _____ Well, I'll

see you a - round, I'll see you a - round. Na na na na na!

*Vocal tacet on repeat*

# HAPPINESS LOVES COMPANY

Words and Music by ANTHONY KIEDIS,
FLEA, CHAD SMITH
and JOSH KLINGHOFFER

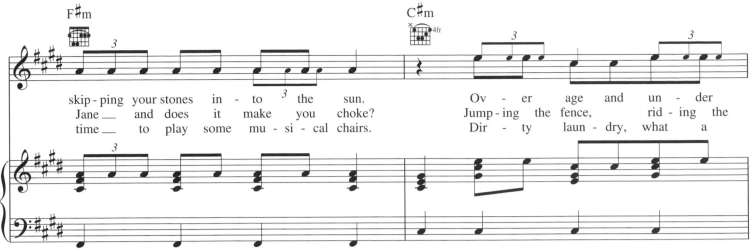

skip - ping your stones in - to the sun.
Jane __ and does it make you choke?
time __ to play some mu - si - cal chairs.

Ov - er age and un - der
Jump - ing the fence, rid - ing the
Dir - ty laun - dry, what a

thumb, ah does it weigh a ton?
rails, oh can you take a joke?
quan - dry, ask her if she cares.

I'll be yours to - night,
I'll be yours to - day,
I'll be yours and more,

liv - ing the dream of a me - te - or - ite!
liv - ing the dream with a ca - pi - tal K!
bet - ter than ev - er like nev - er be - fore!

Stop jump - ing 'cause

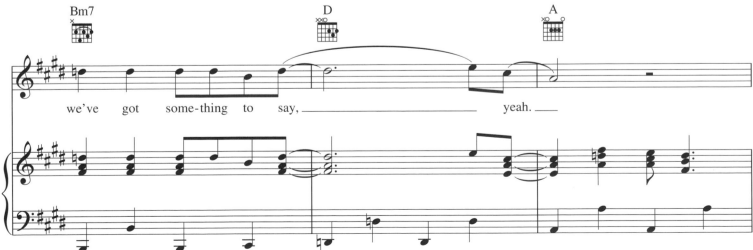

we've got some - thing to say, _____ yeah. __

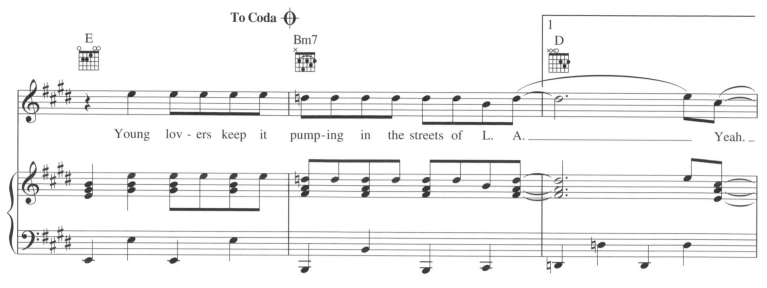

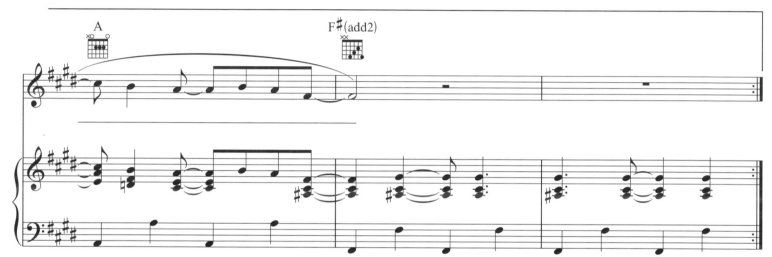

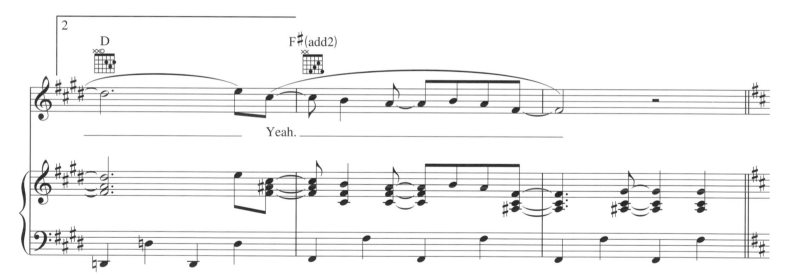

Make time ___ for love and ___ your hap - pi - ness. _____
We all know ___ and strug - gle with ___ some lone - li - ness. _____

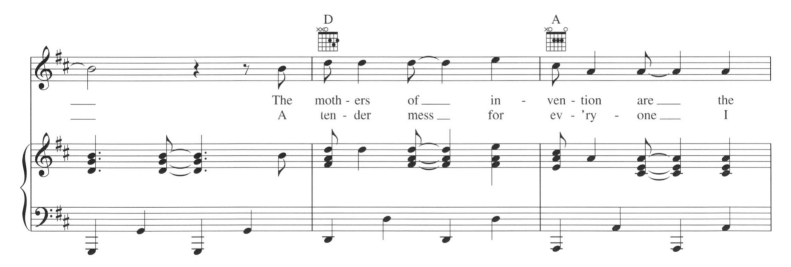

The moth - ers of ____ in - ven - tion are ___ the
A ten - der mess ___ for ev - 'ry - one ___ I

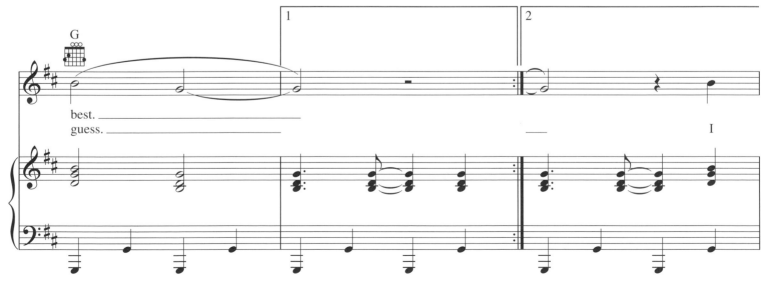

best. _____
guess. _____ I

D.S. al Coda

guess. _____

**CODA**

pump- ing in the streets of L...  Make time __ for love and __ your

We all know __ and strug- gle with __ some

hap - pi - ness. _____ The moth - ers of ___ in-

lone - li - ness. _____ A ten - der mess ___ for

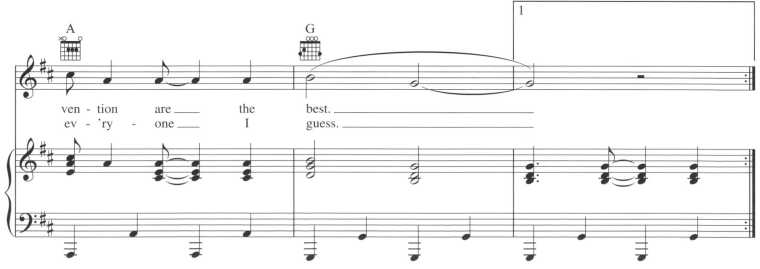

ven - tion are ___ the best. _____

ev - 'ry - one ___ I guess. _____

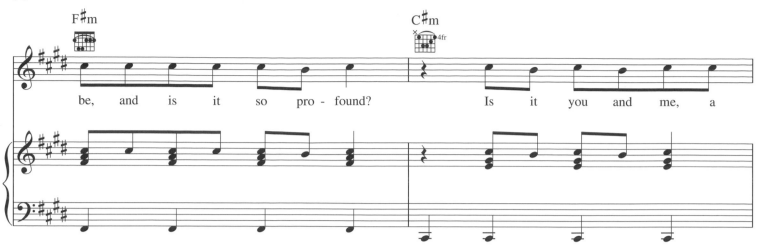

be, and is it so pro - found? Is it you and me, a

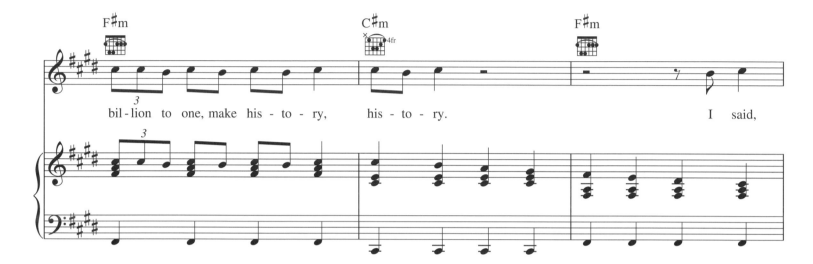

bil - lion to one, make his - to - ry, his - to - ry. I said,

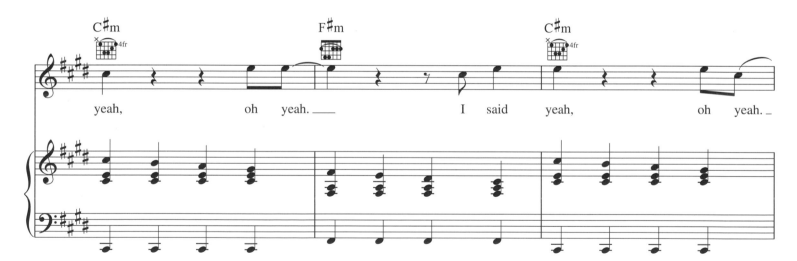

yeah, oh yeah. ___ I said yeah, oh yeah. __

___ I said, oh yeah, oh yeah! ___

# POLICE STATION

Words and Music by ANTHONY KIEDIS,
FLEA, CHAD SMITH
and JOSH KLINGHOFFER

**Moderate Rock**

I

saw you at the po - lice sta - tion and it breaks my heart to say.___ Your

eyes had wan-dered off __ to some - thing dis - tant, cold and grey. __

I guess you did-n't see it com - ing, some-one's got-ten used to slum - ming.

A dream-ing of the gold - en years, __ I see you had to change ca - reers. __ Far __

_____ a - way, __ but we both know __ it's some - where. I

saw you on the back page of ___ some free press yes - ter - day. ___ The
saw you on a T - V sta - tion and it made me want to pray. ___ An
saw you in the church - yard, there ___ was no time to ex - change. ___

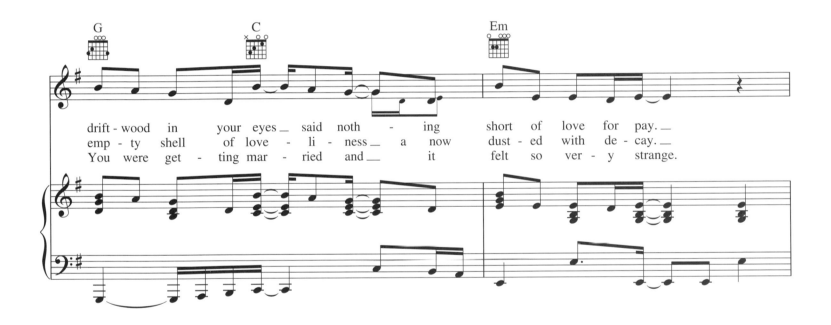

drift - wood in your eyes ___ said noth - ing short of love for pay. ___
emp - ty shell of love - li - ness ___ a now dust - ed with de - cay. ___
You were get - ting mar - ried and ___ it felt so ver - y strange.

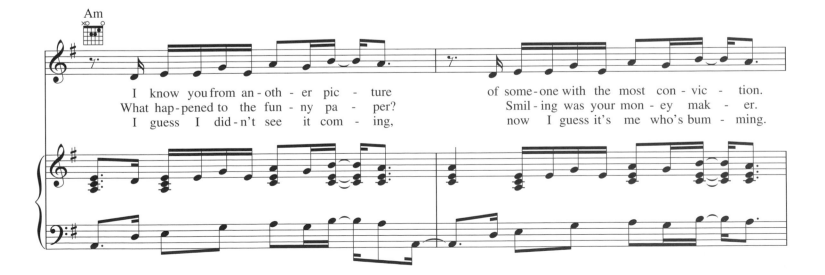

I know you from an - oth - er pic - ture of some - one with the most con - vic - tion.
What hap - pened to the fun - ny pa - per? Smil - ing was your mon - ey mak - er.
I guess I did - n't see it com - ing, now I guess it's me who's bum - ming.

We used to read the fun - ny pa - pers,     a fooled a-round and pulled some ca - pers. Not
Some - one ought to sit - u - ate her,     find a way to ed - u - cate her. All
Dream - ing of the gol - den years,     you and I were mix - ing tears. Not

to - day,     I send a mes - sage to her,
the way,     time to come and find you,
to - day,     not for me but some - one,

a mes - sage that I'm com - ing,     a com - ing to pur - sue her.
you can't hide from me girl so     nev - er mind what I do.
I nev - er could get used to,     so now I will re - fuse to.

Down home coun - try, I _____ rest my face on your _____
Down home coun - try, I _____ rest my face on your _____
Down home coun - try, I _____ rest my face on your _____

bed. Well, I've got you
bed. I've met my
bed. I've met my

ten times o - ver, I'll _____ chase you down _____ 'til you're _____
soul mate coun - try and _____ I left it all _____ for your _____
soul mate coun - try and _____ I left it all _____ for your _____

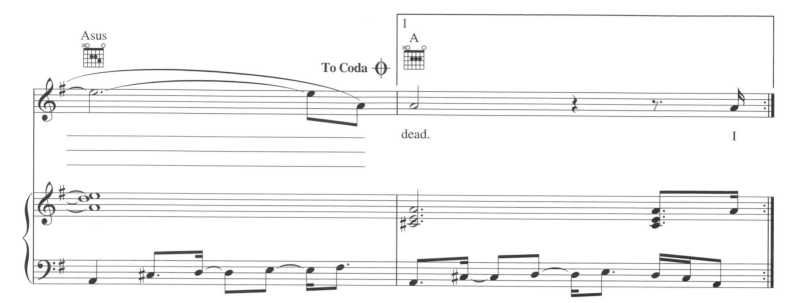

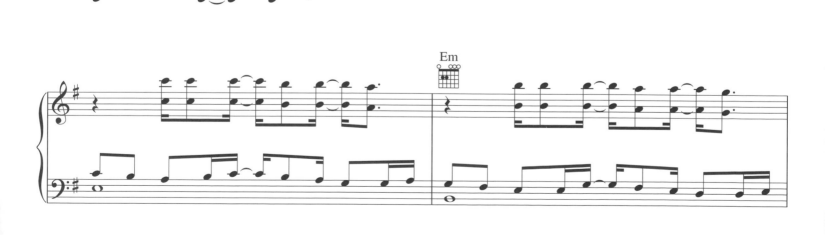

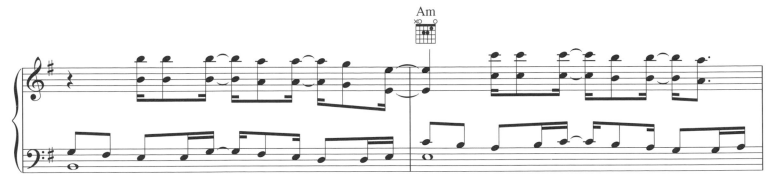

head.                    Well, I've got my best foot for - ward and __

I'll chase you down __ 'til you're __ dead. ____

Play 4 times

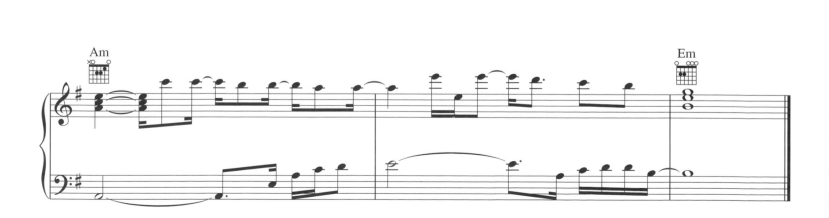

# EVEN YOU BRUTUS?

Words and Music by ANTHONY KIEDIS,
FLEA, CHAD SMITH
and JOSH KLINGHOFFER

Moderate Funk Rock

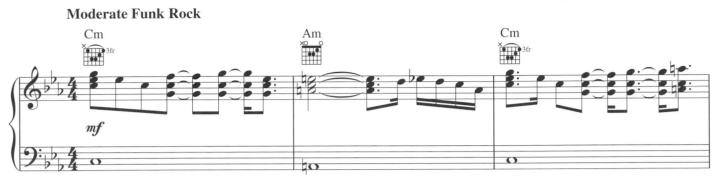

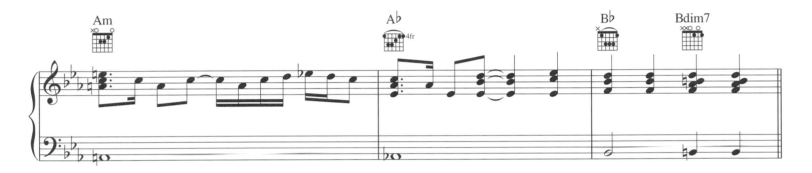

God is good and fate is great, when it feels so strong it's hard to wait. You nev-er know

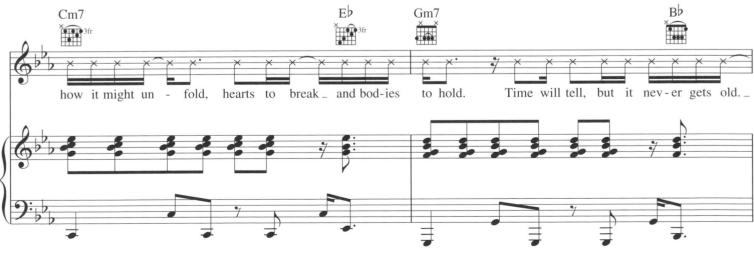

how it might un-fold, hearts to break and bod-ies to hold. Time will tell, but it nev-er gets old.

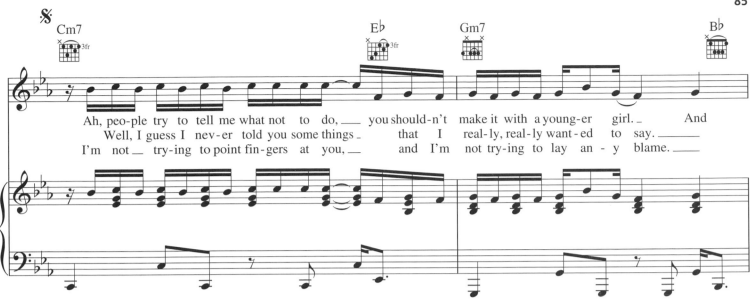

Ah, peo-ple try to tell me what not to do, \_\_\_ you should-n't make it with a young-er girl. \_\_\_ And
Well, I guess I nev-er told you some things \_ that I real-ly, real-ly want-ed to say. _____
I'm not \_ try-ing to point fin-gers at you, \_ and I'm not try-ing to lay an - y blame. \_\_\_\_

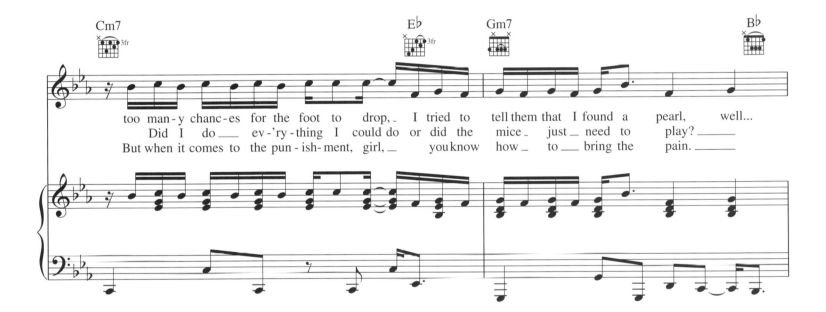

too man - y chanc-es for the foot to drop, \_ I tried to tell them that I found a pearl, well...
Did I do \_\_\_ ev-'ry-thing I could do or did the mice \_ just \_ need to play? _____
But when it comes to the pun-ish-ment, girl, \_ you know how \_ to \_ bring the pain. _____

Like I told \_\_\_ you, be \_\_\_\_\_ care - ful what you're ask - ing for.
Like I told \_\_\_ you, there's more \_\_\_\_\_ than \_\_\_ meets the eye.
Like I told \_\_\_ you, I'd \_\_\_\_\_ do \_\_\_ it \_\_\_\_\_ all a - gain.

Hey, sis-ter Bru-tus, got a mess_ of a bet-ter half. _

_ Oh. _ Hey, sis-ter Ju-das, e - ven

you nev-er had my back. _ _

# MEET ME AT THE CORNER

Words and Music by ANTHONY KIEDIS,
FLEA, CHAD SMITH
and JOSH KLINGHOFFER

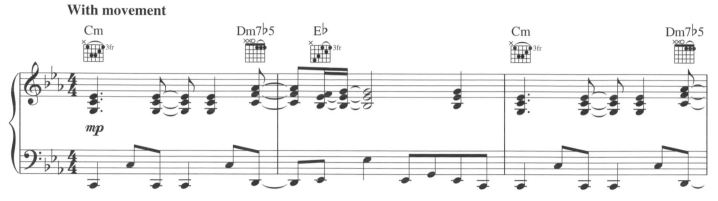

Please don't ask me who, \_\_\_\_\_
Please don't ask me where, \_\_\_\_\_
Please don't say you want \_\_\_\_\_

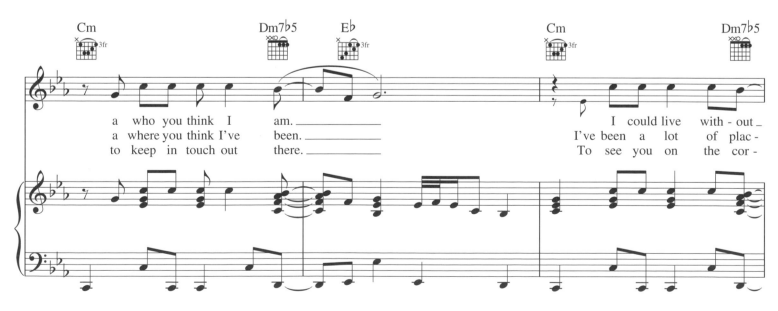

a who you think I     am. _____          I could live     with - out \_
a where you think I've been. _____          I've been a lot     of plac -
to keep in touch out     there. _____          To see you on     the cor -

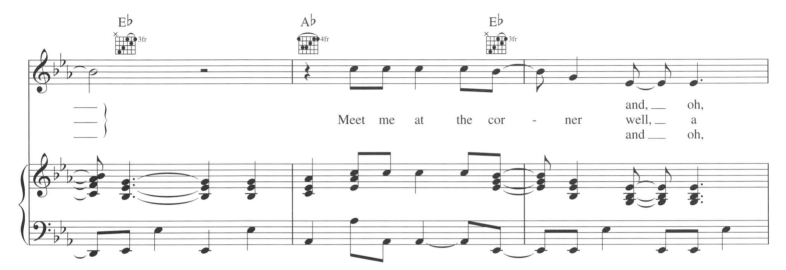

To Coda ⊕

Re-ced-ing in-to the for - est, I ___ will lay a - round and wait, ___

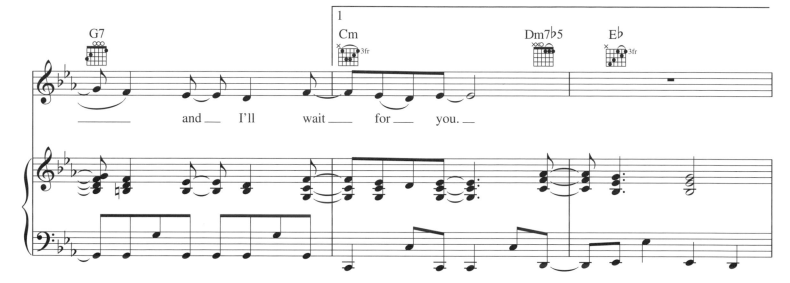

___ and ___ I'll wait ___ for ___ you. ___

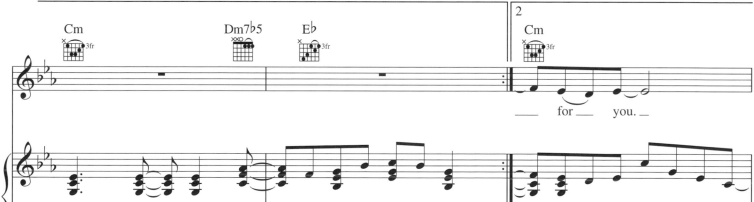

___ for ___ you. ___

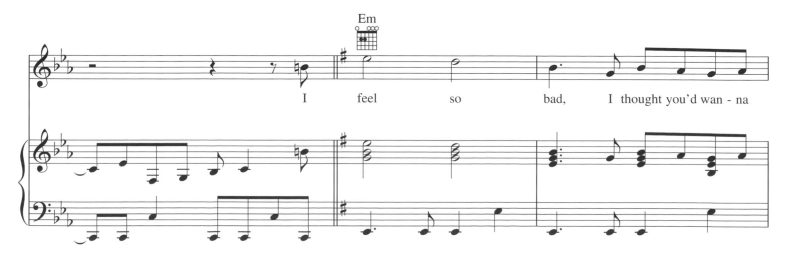

I feel so bad, I thought you'd wan - na

know. _____ Well, I feel so

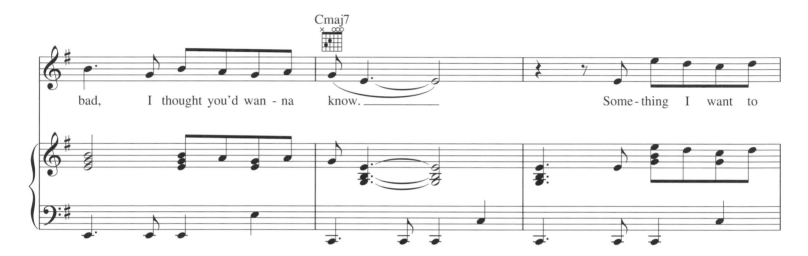

bad, I thought you'd wan - na know. _____ Some - thing I want to

show, _____ I thought you ought to know. _____

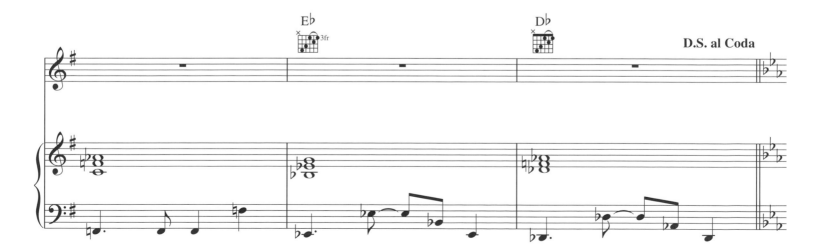

D.S. al Coda

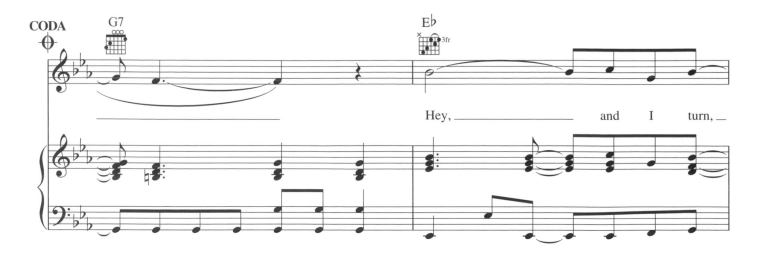

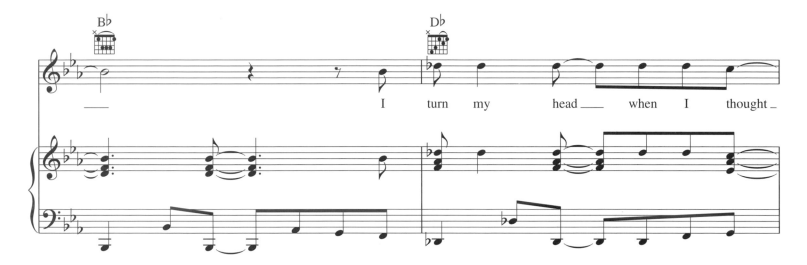

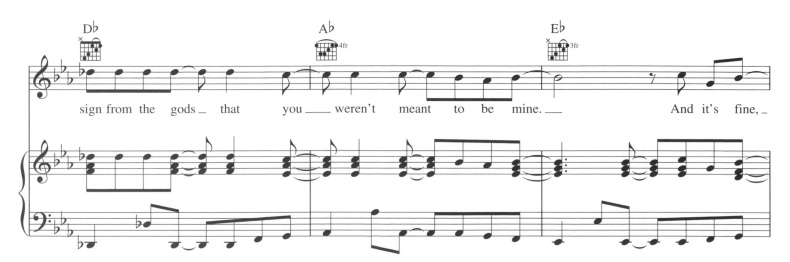

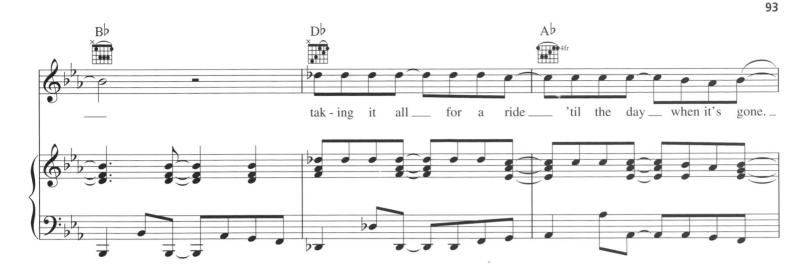

tak-ing it all___ for a ride___ 'til the day___ when it's gone.___

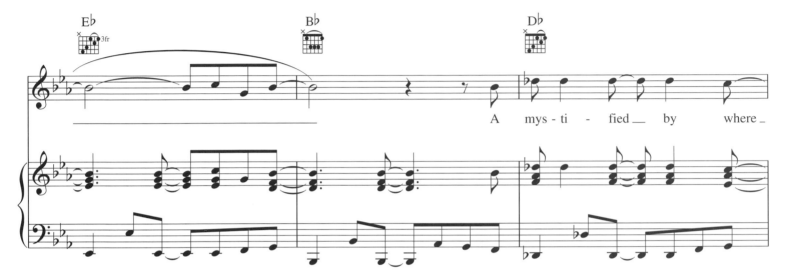

_____ A mys-ti - fied___ by where___

___ it all_____ went wrong_____ when it's gone.___ I

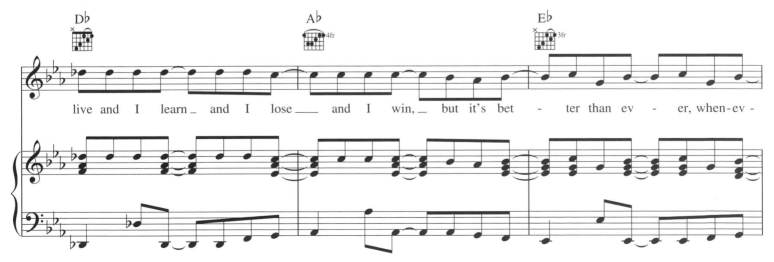

live and I learn___ and I lose___ and I win,___ but it's bet - ter than ev - er, when-ev -

-er I'm in. ___ Thank you, girl ___ for ev - 'ry - where ___ that we've

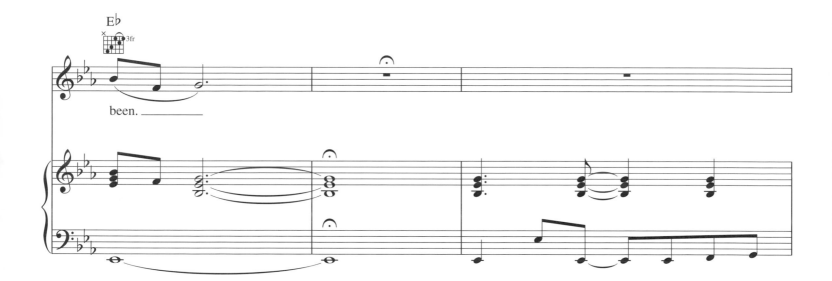

been. _____

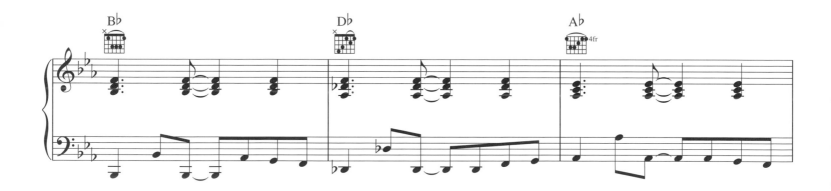

# DANCE, DANCE, DANCE

Words and Music by ANTHONY KIEDIS,
FLEA, CHAD SMITH
and JOSH KLINGHOFFER

**Syncopated groove**

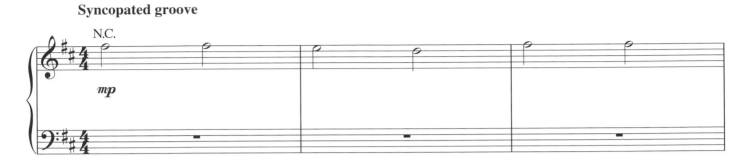

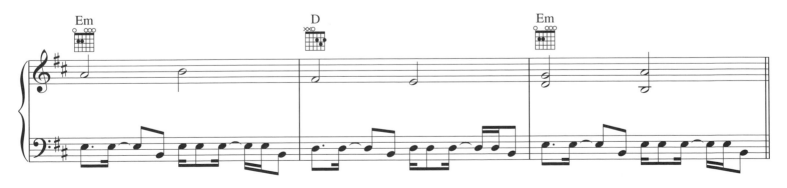

You got yours __ and I've got mine, __ she got his __ and she got shine. __
They got this __ and we got that, __ he got his __ and she got fat. __

Un-der moon and o-ver-seas, __ she's got those __ and we got these. __
You got mine __ but I got yours, I got love __ but you've got more. __

Dance, dance, dance, dance all night long, __ yes all night long. __

Dance, dance, dance, dance, we got strong, __ yes we got strong. __ Let's

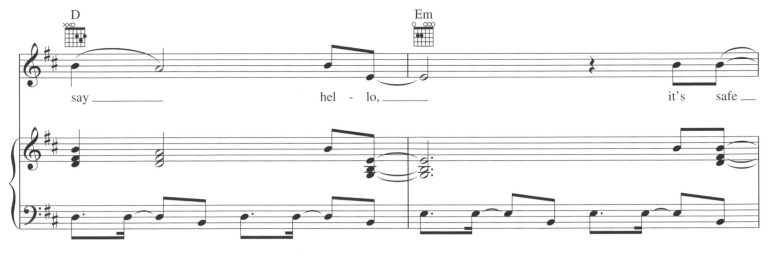

say _____ hel - lo, _____ it's safe \_\_\_

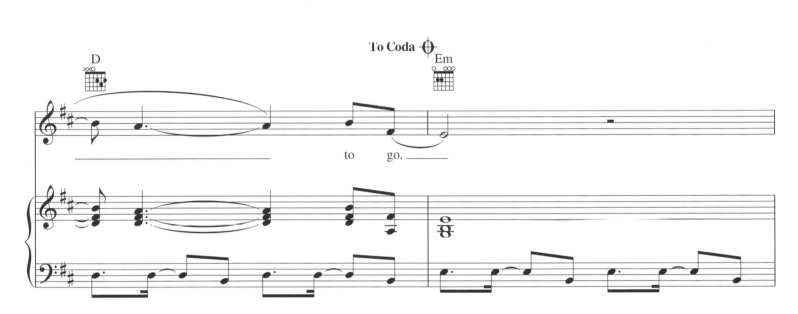

**To Coda** ⊕

_____ to go. _____

Dance, dance, dance, dance all night long\_ and all night long.\_

Dance, dance, dance, dance, we got strong,\_ yes we got strong.\_ The

light _____ _____ is right, _____ let's play _____

_____ to - night, _____ let's

play.

Give your - self _____ a chance _____ to find _____

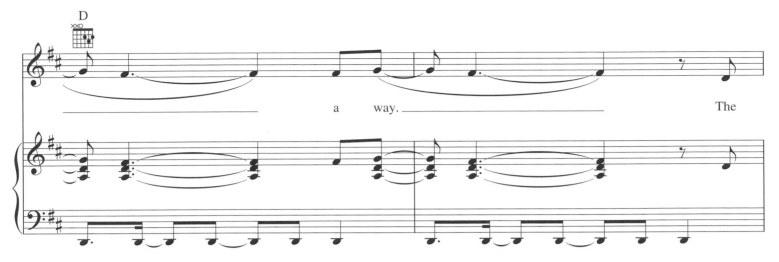

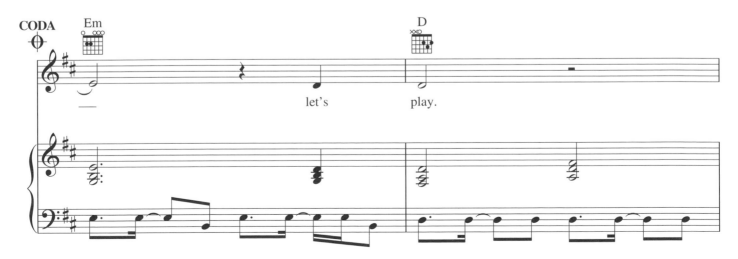

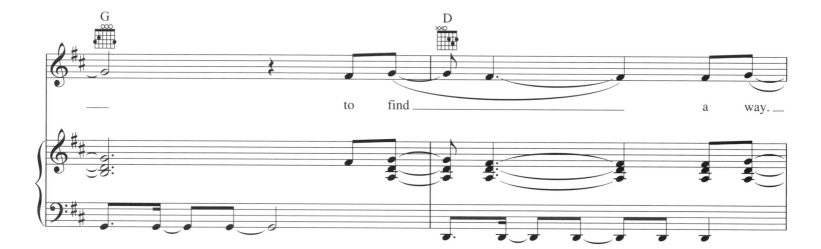

Tell your ___ mom ___ and dad ___

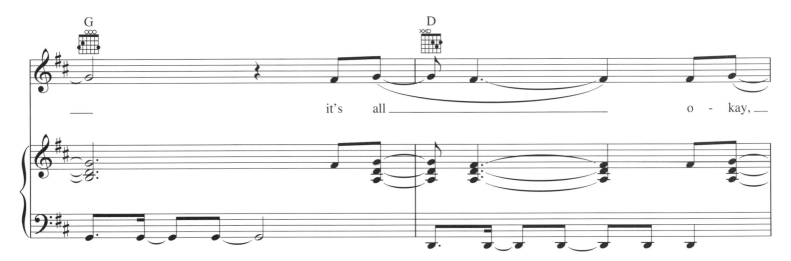

___ it's all ___ o - kay, ___

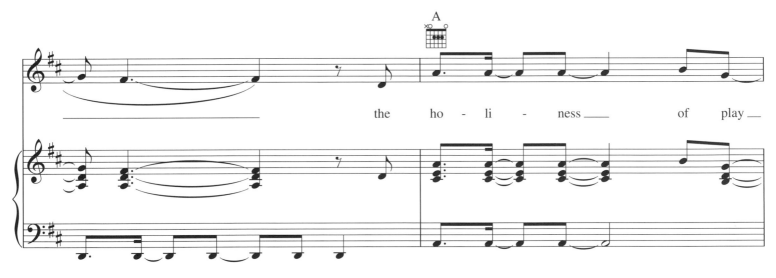

___ the ho - li - ness ___ of play ___

___ is here ___ to stay. ___

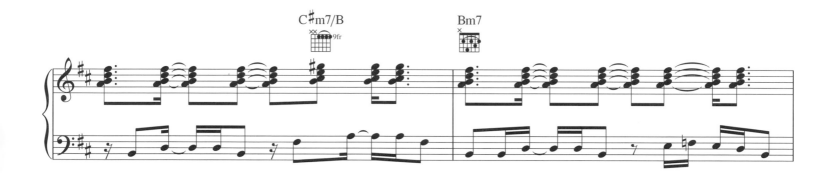

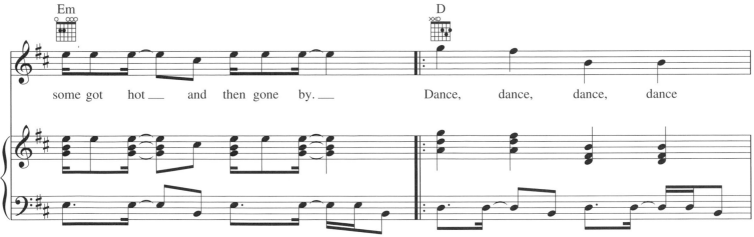

some got hot ___ and then gone by. ___ Dance, dance, dance, dance

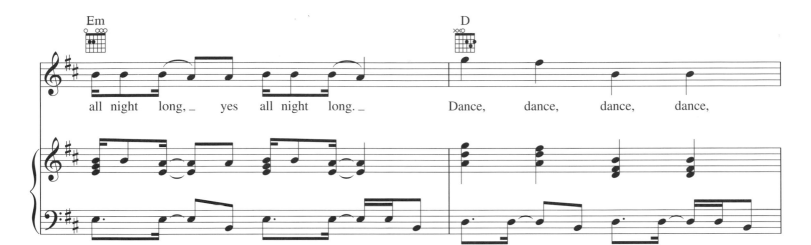

all night long, ___ yes all night long. ___ Dance, dance, dance, dance,

we've got strong, ___ yes we've got strong. We say ___ hel - lo, ___
The light ___ is right, ___

___ it's safe ___ to go.
___ lift here ___ to - night, ___

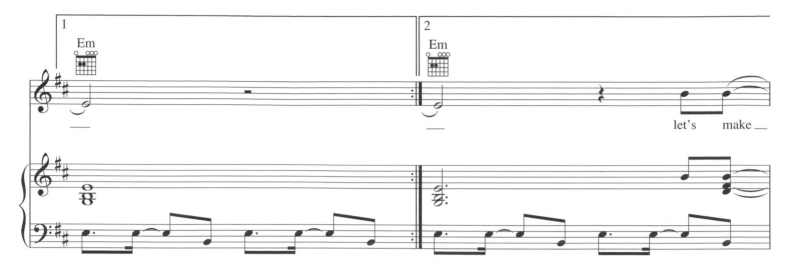

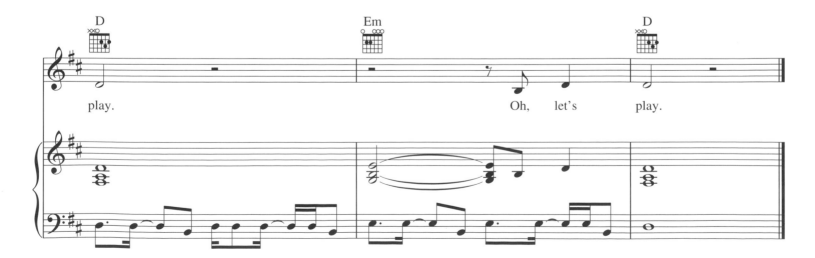